TURNING
INTUITION
— INTO —
SCIENCE

Harnessing the Power of Organizational Network Analysis

DEBORAH PECK, Ph.D.

Publishing support provided by
Ignite Press
5070 N. Sixth St. #189
Fresno, CA 93710
www.IgnitePress.us

ISBN: 979-8-9885105-0-5
ISBN: 979-8-9885105-1-2 (Hardcover)
ISBN: 979-8-9885105-2-9 (E-book)

For bulk purchase and for booking, contact:

Deborah Peck
dpeck@seity.com
http://www.seity.com

Library of Congress Control Number: 2023909254

Cover design by Nathaniel Dasco
Edited by Charlie Wormhoudt
Interior design by Jetlaunch

FIRST EDITION

To Keith and Ryan,
with much love, appreciation, and
heartfelt thanks for being there for me—always.

TABLE OF CONTENTS

AUTHOR'S NOTE

At the start of my journey as an Industrial/Organizational Psychologist, I realized I needed something to distinguish myself among the masses of consultants. Eventually, I found Social Network Analysis (SNA). To apply it to organizations, it was called Organizational Network Analysis (ONA).

After intense research, I realized ONA was a valuable diagnostic tool for the kind of work I wanted to do for organizations. I didn't realize it was unknown to most business leaders. Once I decided that was the focus for my business, I started to develop how best to offer it to clients.

I had a lot of work to do to educate decision makers and market something that wasn't a product. It was a service that used science. It had to be explained in business terms and related to what would appeal to decision makers for organizational effectiveness and organization health.

I won't go into all the failed attempts and frustrating moments. To think that something this important and valuable for organizations was not obvious to leaders when I met with them puzzled me at first. It was going to take time.

It reminded me of the technology start-up companies I worked in before changing careers. If it is worth it, it takes patience, time, and education for leaders. I spent a lot of time explaining the value and purpose of ONA. Along with that came sunken costs in development, marketing, and sales.

I was motivated to develop my brand and reputation in a new field. I was on a mission to gain exposure so I could share ONA with the business community. I developed relationships and a strong network that I continue to rely upon.

This book is a tangible result of the path I took, the people that supported me along the way, and the clients that found ONA valuable for their organizations. They all contributed to my work and got me to the point of sharing their stories with you through this book.

You will read client stories that you might relate to and gain something useful for your own experience and workplace. I hope you benefit from the stories of leaders who have experienced ONA benefits and improved their organizations as a result.

I must share one person that impacted how I looked at this important tool for organizations and leaders. He is mentioned in the Acknowledgements as well. Jack Milligan is a well-known HR professional. When I presented ONA to his company, Jack got up out of his chair and leaned across the table.

He said, "Where have you been hiding? This is fantastic and something every HR person and key decision-makers in organizations should know about and use. This closes the gap between how we look at the organization and what is really happening in the workplace. This turns intuition into science!"

Yes, it is Jack Milligan who coined the phrase and generously gave me permission to use it for my tag line. It only makes sense to me that it is the title of my book. Thank you, Jack! You supported me throughout my career and are one of my biggest fans. I appreciate it, and you, very much!

As an Industrial/Organizational Psychologist, I wanted to learn and use ONA to expand I/O Psychology research and perspectives related to the organization/workplace. A lot of Psychology research and literature took a more individual view.

There was very little mention of ONA in my discipline, other than in Social Psychology. With ONA, I thought I could contribute and help advance my discipline and contribute to organizational effectiveness.

INTRODUCTION

"The 'trick' is to develop formal mathematical definitions that have known graph theoretic properties, and also capture important intuitive and theoretical aspects of cohesive subgroups."

—KATHERINE FAUST

How to Get the Most from This Book

Welcome, and please explore the pages to learn about a valuable method to understand your workplace and organization! I invite you to experience Organizational Network Analysis (ONA) through the stories of clients that I have supported and worked with over the years.

I wrote this book for leaders, decision makers, business professionals, and anyone curious to learn more about people networks, the informal and emerging networks in your organizations. Although not new, ONA is still relatively unknown to many in the business world. This book guides you to apply it to business problems and decisions that others have faced, and that you might be facing as well.

I have been on a journey in my consulting practice to educate, coach, and support leaders, both formal and informal, to bring network analysis to organizations. ONA is a "have to have" diagnostic for every organization. You will learn why that is true. It is a form of people analytics, but broader and deeper in how it is used and what it uncovers.

The stories I share will demonstrate how work really gets done. ONA results yield surprising insights or might validate what you already know, or suspect is happening. That is your intuition. Using ONA in the workplace is about *turning intuition into science.*

I will explain how ONA analyzes and quantifies the social capital that defines the organization and the culture. Social capital is about the relationships and interdependencies people form to be included, successful, and productive in the workplace. It is about sharing tacit knowledge and information that we can now measure with ONA.

I also explain that it doesn't stop there. Social capital turbocharges the human capital that most organizations are devoted to understanding more deeply. Human capital is typically what people analytics focuses on. ONA brings you a multiplier effect for individual talent and goes beyond what we commonly value, which are knowledge, skills, and abilities (KSAs). The KSAs of every individual are important for developing an effective workforce and organization but they are not enough.

The truth of what really happens is in how individuals interact, build relationships, and form interdependencies that improve, create, or ignore processes and procedures. They find more efficient methods to complete their tasks, obtain information, develop expertise, or seek advice. They determine who they can work with based on the task at hand, trust, expertise, function, need, or other factors.

Leaders are looking for methods to value and enhance human capital for many reasons such as retention, engagement, collaboration, culture, and to support and meet their business objectives. The value of individual employees is measured using human capital metrics such as productivity and retention metrics, and methods such as behavioral assessments, succession planning, and performance reviews.

From an ONA perspective, that is one part of the equation and a start. There is power in the emerging informal networks that ONA makes visible, real, and substantive so you can measure, see, and act based on the results. I will explain how human capital and social capital combine to create employee value, which creates norms, the culture, productivity, and organizational effectiveness.

- Have you been searching to understand your organization more fully as a system?
- Are there symptoms of issues that you aren't sure what to do about?
- Do you have recurring problems that you can't seem to solve?
- Does communication and collaboration help or hinder organizational effectiveness?
- Do you think there are unsolvable mysteries to effectively integrate departments, companies, groups, or cultures after an acquisition or organizational restructuring?
- Is stagnating innovation stopping you from gaining a competitive advantage in your industry or market?

These are just some of the questions that are answered in the stories you will read. Each chapter involves a different topic with some that include multiple topics. At the start of each chapter, there is an overview that gives you a quick understanding of the client problem, why the client opted to use ONA, what we did, and the outcomes. Throughout each chapter, there are graphs/ maps to explain concepts in color.

Here is a thumbnail summary of each chapter in case you have a specific topic in mind to explore further related to applying ONA.

Communication, Trust, Engagement

Chapter 2 is a story about using ONA for an IT department in a Healthcare organization for a Fortune 10 company. The CIO was experiencing some communication and retention issues. He thought he knew what the issue was for his organization. ONA found something different that employee engagement survey results validated.

Organizational Structure, Strategy, Communication

Chapter 3 shares the story of a CEO who struggled to align the operating company presidents for an enterprise strategy. He found ONA useful to "enlighten" the company presidents and make progress in developing a strategy to gain alignment. Another ONA process identified the key communicators across the enterprise that improved employee engagement.

Collaboration and Gender Balance

Chapter 4 shares an example of using ONA during the pandemic for an IT department in a healthcare company. They were having difficulties with employee engagement and the culture because of a previous restructuring and some other issues. Data from employee opinion surveys combined with ONA results to develop positive change initiatives.

Career Path, Knowledge Transfer, and Generational Differences

Chapter 5 is a story about a manufacturing company that develops, tests, manufactures, and sells pyrotechnic and energetic products to airlines and other industries. They have chemists and engineers that develop these products. The CEO and the engineering division HR VP were developing a knowledge transfer program before many management baby boomers retired. As it turned out, there were several key findings about generational differences, career paths, and improvements for the knowledge transfer plans.

Organizational Change

Chapter 6 is about a healthcare DME and infusion company that was going through change. They had a new executive team and had acquired the infusion company a few years before. Lingering challenges came to light with the new CEO and the focus on change and ONA. ONA provided information they didn't know about related to the integration of both companies and identified the change agents.

Culture and Values

Chapter 7 discusses a first responder organization facing mass exits through resignations and/or retirements with about 64% of the workforce retiring in 5–6 years. The leader was concerned about the culture, values, employee retention, and the institutional knowledge leaving the organization. They chose ONA to understand the breadth and depth of the employee exits and the impact on the organization. The information was used to support changes in recruiting, selection, training, promotions and employee development ideas and processes.

Mergers and Acquisitions

Chapter 8 uses examples from two of the other chapter stories to demonstrate the value of ONA for a merger and acquisition to integrate two cultures. The two examples come from the healthcare company that used ONA for organizational change management (from Chapter 6) and the first responder organization that used it to identify emerging leaders and power brokers to support positive change (from Chapter 9).

Emerging Leaders, Power Brokers, Change Agents, and Path for Improvement

Chapter 9 is about another first responder organization that was experiencing some employee unrest, an upcoming change in the executive ranks, and uncertainty about how a previous acquisition affected their culture and leadership plans. It was important for them to identify emerging leaders, change agents, and the power brokers in the organization to support and create positive change.

Use ONA to turn your intuition into science. Get an objective understanding of how the work is really done in your organization. Be willing to learn that your view might only be what is on the surface. ONA gives you a complete picture, in-depth analysis, and supporting metrics to make changes, make informed decisions, and take your organization forward with confidence.

PART ONE:

ORGANIZATIONAL NETWORK ANALYSIS 101

1

AN INTRODUCTION TO ORGANIZATIONAL NETWORK ANALYSIS (ONA)

PICTURE THIS. YOU just completed a major software upgrade in your organization, and you think that two of the major groups that should be working together and communicating effectively are not. What do you do? Are you sure this is what is happening? How do you really know? Maybe others have told you that it is happening, maybe you have observed it in some way in passing or overheard a discussion about it. Or maybe you think you know what is happening since you are an experienced leader and that is your responsibility. Your intuition is at work.

This situation is what one leader in a healthcare organization faced and identified as a communication problem between two major groups in his department. The two groups needed to work together effectively to ensure a major software change was implemented and used successfully in their systems and processes to support the business. The leader thought a custom team-building workshop would help resolve the communication issues.

Before taking the time to develop the custom workshop and use the budget for a solution that might only be a temporary solution, I suggested an Organizational Network Analysis (ONA) first. Communication might have been a symptom, but was it the problem? ONA often uncovers the root cause of a problem that a leader is experiencing or has dealt with for a long time.

As it turned out, the issue wasn't communication between the two groups. Instead, it was a trust issue among all the managers in the department. That affected communication but not the way the leader thought for the non-management employees. Read the full details of this in Chapter 3.

> *The people within your organization are speaking to you through their behavior, how they work with others and what they naturally offer to your organization. ONA makes their messages visible, measurable, and actionable.*

Do you have an issue in your organization that doesn't seem to go away? Have you searched for answers and tried different methods thinking they would resolve the issue but didn't? Are you looking for methods for your organization to improve collaboration, information and knowledge sharing, and really know what is happening in the workplace that affects organization health?

Maybe ONA will be the method that will help you find the root cause of the issue and offer you an avenue to overcome it. The people within your organization are speaking to you through their behavior, how they work with others, and what they naturally offer to your organization. ONA makes their messages visible, measurable, and actionable.

Many of the stories in this book address issues that leaders like you struggle with or perhaps have had for a long time. When these leaders learned about ONA, they often realized they might have been looking at the issue in the wrong way, or were trying to solve the wrong problem. ONA gave them clarity on what they thought was occurring and told them what was really happening.

It gives you a visual understanding and supporting metrics that confirm the analysis.

ONA is a scientifically researched, diagnostic method that identifies, measures, and analyzes the social capital in the workplace. ONA uses Social Network Analysis (SNA) principles and supporting theories to apply the method as a diagnostic for organizations. Using SNA in organizations is called ONA.

Social Network Analysis (SNA) is the process of analyzing social structures using networks and graph theory. It uses relational data to describe the overall network structure in a social system, like an organization or workplace. It can process large amounts of this data to analyze relationships in the network and what they mean.

In an organization, ONA makes the invisible visible by using graphs, which are called maps, to show interactions among people in the organization. These people are called nodes and look like *dots* on the map. The graphs are developed using software designed to calculate the connections between people.

The connections are based on responses/interactions and the value of the relationship. The value of the relationship depends on the purpose and frequency of their connection. The purpose might be work, innovation, expertise, or other topics which can be measured and used to map out a *network* specific to each purpose. There will be more information about the specific networks in the stories.

How Can ONA Be Used

ONA is used to help organizations evaluate and analyze the white space on the organization chart (org chart). What is really happening in the organization? How is the work really getting done? Do we really know who is making a difference in our organization? This can be determined using ONA, but that is only the start.

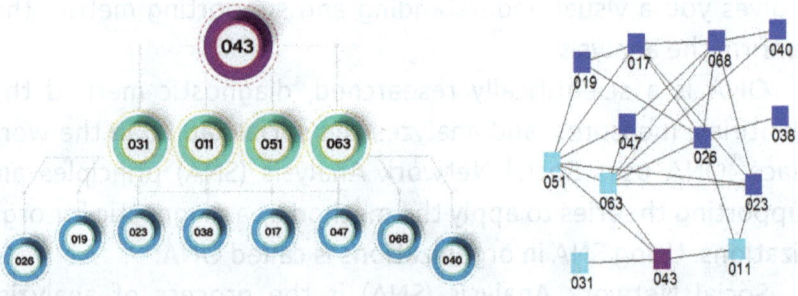

The org chart (above) is typically how we visualize the organization. It provides an explicit view of the reporting structure of the organization, which is based on function. It specifies who reports to whom, what function they provide, and the reporting structure to make decisions.

The org chart doesn't address how people really interact, form relationships, and work together to accomplish their daily tasks and goals to fulfill their assigned function. The map/graph on the right is how the work is really done in the organization. ONA provides the visual interpretation of how the work is done in your organization. ONA tells you what is happening to fill in the white space on the org chart.

There is usually a one-to-one connection for the reporting structure in the organization. That creates a lot of white space, which isn't an accurate representation since the work doesn't happen between the two people in the one-to-one connection alone. People reach out to others to find experts, get an answer more quickly, get a task completed more easily, or find ways to improve how they work.

For example, we can use the org chart on the left and the ONA interpretation on the right to understand the white space ONA makes explicit.

- Look at node 063 in the org chart. This leader has direct reports 047, 068, and 040. In the actual work and information flow, 063 is also connected to 023 and 026 as well as peer node 051, and the CEO at the top, 043.

- Leader node 051 has only one direct report, 017, but also connects to nodes 019, 047, and 023 as well as peer node 063 and the CEO 043.
- Leader node 031 is likely the most interesting to explore since this person makes a conscious decision to only connect to the CEO 043. They don't even share information and workflow with their direct reports, 023, 019, and 026. Those employees are getting their information and directions from leaders 051 or 063.

What do you think the impact would be to alignment, decision-making, problem solving or other important actions within this organization when 031 only communicates with the CEO? What about the influence that 063 and 051 have overall on the organization? Do you think that is recognized by the CEO if he/she didn't have the benefit of ONA? Who do you think holds the most social capital among the top leaders in this organization?

ONA addresses organizational change, communication, collaboration, innovation, improvement, development, restructuring, and much more. ONA develops a picture of your organization from a macro/systems view. It also includes a micro view of individuals or groups to determine the social capital or influence they might have.

The science involved includes metrics to interpret the results. The research and science behind SNA and ONA provide an objective understanding of what is really happening in the workplace. This type of diagnostic was not available before SNA/ONA. If you think you know what is happening or who people interact with, ONA will either validate it or find exceptions and information you likely didn't know about.

Organizations often use human capital information they have collected through a variety of assessments or observations and interactions with employees. However, in most cases, decision makers develop a lot of assumptions and use their intuition to make evaluations and decisions and to solve problems. Sometimes they are right but not always. They end up making subjective decisions about important issues that involve or are about people.

I use ONA to "turn intuition into science" so you can *see* the organization in a different way and fill in the white space on the org chart. ONA identifies and analyzes the social capital in an organization. Identifying social capital in organizations is the missing link to objectively understanding and healing organizations.

> *Think of ONA like an X-ray of your organization. The X-ray makes [the problem] visible for the doctor to isolate, confirm, and diagnose in order to determine the severity. The X-ray helps the doctor figure out options and the best solution(s) to fix the broken bone or problem.*

There aren't many tools or methods that analyze the ecosystem of the organization and can offer you the insight that ONA produces. ONA provides objective data, analysis, metrics, and information about how the organization really functions as a whole system. It also provides details about individuals and their contribution to the system. It does this based on:

- How people interact for different reasons—for example, innovation, improvement, strategy
- How people develop relationships to get their jobs done—who they depend on
- How people collaborate, build the culture, and create norms they work by to meet goals and objectives

Think of ONA like an X-ray of your organization. You go to the doctor with some type of problem, and you might have an idea what the problem is and how it was caused. The doctor orders an X-ray to find out more. For example, you might have a broken bone. The X-ray doesn't repair the broken bone. The X-ray makes it visible for the doctor to isolate, confirm, and diagnose in order to determine the severity. The X-ray helps the doctor figure out options and the best solution(s) to fix the broken bone. It also indicates other issues to consider that could be affected in some way by the diagnosis and solution(s).

ONA does the same thing as the X-ray. ONA:

- Displays an X-ray of how your organization is functioning today
- Provides an overview of the organization as a whole—how the system is working today
- Shows where people are collaborating or if they are disconnected in some way
- Shows patterns of communication, workflow, knowledge and information sharing, and collaboration
- Identifies who is involved, who should be but isn't, who is influential, who might be disconnected, who might be a surprise key individual (like a mentor or innovator), and much more
- Identifies the culture carriers, emerging leaders, and power brokers in each network, and the change agents that can affect the organization
- Identifies who might be a bridge to repair or grow the network(s) as you want them
- Provides valuable information to figure out solutions that will stick or indicate dependencies affected

ONA Deliverables

ONA results provide a baseline. You will gain an objective view of how your organization functions. From the results you can make confident, objective decisions and solve problems effectively.

ONA might also clarify information or confirm/contradict what you think is occurring. ONA offers a method to measure change and the opportunity to use the analysis and results for business planning and strategy.

In one example, which you will read about in Chapter 3, ONA validated a CEO's concern that the communication silos between companies in the enterprise he led exemplified executive-level misalignment and restricted strategy collaboration. On the other hand, in the story in Chapter 9, ONA brought good news that the organization had consolidated more successfully than senior leaders had assumed. However, it also pointed out the possible bias of those leaders since the acquired organization was initiating most of the collaboration and communication to integrate the culture.

At a macro level, you get a view of the organization ecosystem and how people collaborate, share information, and work together. At a micro level, ONA identifies the key influencers, change agents, emerging leaders, and power brokers in your organization—those people that make or break major initiatives or are enhancing projects or the culture.

> *People networks can make or break changes, enhance innovation, show you clues to the competitive advantage of your industry, and mitigate integration issues from a restructuring or merger and acquisition.*

You likely don't know the impact of how people interact, and if you do, ONA validates your intuition. It identifies valuable and rich data about what is important to people to do their jobs effectively. The competitive advantage, productivity enhancements, and much more for any business lies within these networks.

It is critical to pay attention to the networks in your organization. They can make or break change, enhance innovation, show you clues to the competitive advantage of your industry, and mitigate integration issues from a restructuring or merger and acquisition. People networks are the secret sauce of your organization and help you understand how employees make contributions to the whole through their social capital.

The Importance of ONA

I recently presented a short introduction about ONA to a group of undergraduate students. I was asked to be a guest speaker by their instructor to talk about organizational change management and how ONA supports it. When I finished, one of the students said, "I think every organization and leader should use ONA to help them understand what really happens in their workplace." All I could do was smile and agree. He seemed to get the "have to have" vs. "nice to have" concept I had been trying to achieve with business leaders for years.

Lessons from Leadership That Relate to ONA

There was a career changing lesson about leadership that I learned toward the end of my technology career. When I started my last career move in technology with a local start-up, I was interviewed by one of the founders. They created a leading-edge technology that advanced the Internet substantially. Technology and engineers were the core of the business. This company was a competitor to the leading designers and implementers of the Internet at the time and we had their attention.

We were a Tier 1 Internet Service Provider (ISP) and we had the cream of the crop of engineers and systems programmers. What I faced was that most of the engineers were very young and self-taught or had on-the-job training rather than any engineering formal education. They were mavericks. They were difficult to manage and lead and the founder didn't have the skills or patience to do so. He had already gone through four male directors in three years before I was recommended to him.

I had to clarify ambiguity and find some structure or understanding of the situation to make sense of what I was facing. This really is what ONA does and how I use it to support the organizations I work with—to clarify ambiguity and make sense of what they are facing. I knew nothing about ONA at this point in my career.

Leadership Lesson 1

On my first day, there was no onboarding. I briefly met with my new boss and he gave me one week to get a foundational understanding of the organization. I was to report back to him what I would do with the team, the strategy I had overall to be effective in this position, and what plan I had to move forward.

There were no manuals or resources for me to start to understand the job or to learn anything. I remember finding an empty cube and looking for someone that could give me some clue about where to start or who to talk to. Talk about ambiguity.

I started asking questions of people who walked by to find out more about the organization, my job and who I would be working with. Eventually someone gave me a bit more information, a couple of manuals they knew about, and the names of everyone that would report to me.

During the four days I had before I was to meet with my boss again, I scheduled one-on-one meetings with every engineer that would report to me. There were at least 15–20. They confirmed that they had several bosses before me. None of those previous directors had ever asked them what they did, what they wanted to do, or why they were part of this organization. I did.

It never dawned on me to do anything different. It was my style to listen openly to people, hear what they had to say, strive to understand them and what they did, and let them know that

I valued their contribution to what we had to do. At the time, I didn't realize the true value of that style to prepare me for what I do now.

They were all open and engaged. They told me in-depth information with specifics I could use and drew a lot of diagrams to help me learn faster. They all thanked me, but it was me thanking them for speeding up my learning curve. I think that is why I like and use ONA. It does the same thing using data and metrics and clarifies ambiguity. It speeds up the learning with diagrams and in-depth information about what is really happening and how the work is done.

What I learned was the value of developing relationships, listening with interest, caring about who employees were and what they did, and showing them who I was as a person and as a leader. I asked a lot of questions. Another aspect of leadership learning. It is okay to ask questions. You don't have to be the expert, they are. They all shared openly and were generous with their time. I was building trust.

Leadership includes listening, being okay with not knowing all the answers, connecting with people, and building trust. It is also important to gain a complete picture of employees' contributions to the organization to have objective and valid information to make decisions and solve problems effectively. That is what ONA does.

ONA goes beyond skills and abilities alone or what you can figure out from a resume. It offers a complete picture of how the organization functions based on people interacting together and how they contribute to the organization.

> *Trust is a key factor that ONA helps to understand at a high level. Trust is the glue that holds a relationship together and creates the strength of the relationship in the workplace.*

Leadership Lesson 2

The other thing I learned was that I didn't have to know all the details about what the employees did. However, I did have to relate to them both technically and personally. I had to know enough to call BS on them. I did that too and over time they trusted me. That was another thing I learned—the importance of trust from an employee perspective.

Trust is a key factor that ONA helps to understand at a high level. Trust is the glue that holds a relationship together and creates the strength of the relationship in the workplace. Trust carried me through my career but especially during my time at this company. It really was tested when we were acquired.

It was this last experience, before I left technology as a career and transitioned to what I do now, that cemented for me the importance of listening and really hearing what employees thought and felt. ONA is a way of listening to employees objectively.

Through the ONA process, people answer questions about who they work with, why, and how frequently. ONA provides an open, objective method to "hear" what the employees are telling you and explain what is important to them.

Listening seems simple and it can be if you know how to do it effectively. However, for many managers, it isn't something they think about, or realize the importance of. Often, they are too busy and perhaps ignore what is right in front of them. They might miss what their employees are telling them.

ONA delivers information to you in a way that lets you listen to what employees are telling you. ONA often uncovers new or unknown information that leaders might not have if they aren't listening. You can be more effective, build trust, make better decisions, and solve problems that stick. As Jimi Hendrix said, "Knowledge speaks but wisdom listens."

Applying the Lessons

My goal is to help you enhance your organization's effectiveness through the people in your workplace. That includes respecting the employees and understanding the value they contribute to your success and to the organization.

> *ONA is a roadmap for leaders to listen to their employees in a different way than they might know how to, have thought about, or have ever tried to do.*

ONA is the best tool I have found to uncover employee value based on a holistic perspective. It supplies ideas and direction to help organizations improve and succeed. It helps decision makers, like you, understand all employees' value and your organization fully.

ONA takes it a step further than other tools. Employees contribute to the workplace based on their knowledge, skills, and abilities, but they also contribute by working with others, collaborating, and sharing their knowledge. Identifying the value of the whole person and what they contribute through their interactions with others, combined with the values and vision of the organization, creates the culture and norms.

Using ONA opens more possibilities for people to learn to work with each other more effectively and grow the organization and business. ONA is a roadmap for leaders to listen to their employees in a different way than they might know how to, have thought about, or have ever tried to do.

ONA captures information about employee relationships. It is about how they work together, how they depend on each other, who they trust, who they spend time with, and who they collaborate and communicate with on a regular basis. This tells us how they get their jobs done efficiently and productively.

I have had managers tell me, "Oh, I already know who a key influencer in my department is or who they work with and communicate with." Good managers often do have a good sense of that but not to the depth, breadth, and degree that ONA can capture. It is their intuition informing them.

Before ONA, there wasn't a way to "see" and measure how the organization works as a system or how key people affect the system and culture. With ONA, listening doesn't require one-on-one time, although I recommend that as well. You still need to understand the individual and their skills and abilities.

ONA requires an open mind and willingness to find out how the workplace really functions, how the work is done, and who the key people are that are impacting the organization in different ways.

Often, ONA provides insight and information that leaders were unaware of or couldn't access before. It creates awareness for leaders to let go of their biases and embrace the objective feedback from employees that participate in the process. It presents the reality of the organization. You will find these aspects in the stories in later chapters.

In one instance, I developed a list of the power connectors in each network for an organization. In the Advice Network, there was an individual that the executive did not know.

He said, "I am surprised to see his name since he is relatively new. I decided to invite him to an informal meeting to discuss some ideas so I could get to know him and understand why he showed up so prominently in this network. After I met him in person and observed how he interacted with his peers, I now completely understand why he showed up in this network."

Without ONA, that individual might have been overlooked or his contribution to the organization lost.

More Reasons

ONA won't tell you the nitty gritty of what employees do in their jobs or their ability and skills—that is the human capital component that you should already know. If you don't know, you need to spend time learning about your employees since it matters to them that you know what they do.

ONA tells you how they get it done and defines the interdependencies, key network roles, and the reality of the organization from the perspective of all employees. This includes management. It creates a tangible view of your organization and how the system really functions.

Focusing on the people in the workplace has always been a priority for me. It is what makes the best companies great. Companies that don't put people as their priority but emphasize growth, profit, and shareholders first are missing the point. They won't have the desired profit, growth, and happy shareholders without the people being engaged and satisfied with their jobs.

To understand more of why the focus should be on the people and their contributions, listen and watch Simon Sinek's videos that explain this more emphatically and in an entertaining way. Or consider Level 5 leadership from Jim Collins book *Good to Great*. ONA is a great way to understand how your organization functions as an ecosystem and the contributing members that are the people in it. Why not learn what they have to say and what matters to them?

Is ONA for You?

The Whole is Greater Than the Sum of the Parts

As the university student said after learning about ONA, "I think every leader in an organization should find out how their workplace really functions." I agree. Maybe after you read the examples in the stories in Part 2, you will see it is a have-to-have. Let's go through some initial information to help you decide that more quickly.

You likely already have human capital information for all employees. Human capital is essentially the individual information about an employee—their knowledge, skills, and abilities (KSAs) that you reviewed on their resume or found out more about once they were hired. Human capital is important information but isn't enough to understand employee value and what they offer your organization.

To complete the picture of the human capital impact in your organization, use ONA.

ONA identifies the social capital of employees, leaders, groups, and departments and what it looks like for your organization. Social capital supports human capital and makes it explicit. Added to human capital, you will have the whole picture of how employees contribute, and that signifies employee value.

> *Social capital explains relationships developed in the workplace and the interdependencies people develop to be effective in their jobs.*

Social Capital Makes the Difference

Social capital includes the tacit knowledge that people gain as they increase their experience and knowledge about their job responsibilities or advance in their career choice. It includes trust developed while building relationships in the workplace.

It also includes communication, collaboration, information, and knowledge sharing with people in the workplace to support them in their job tasks and objectives. Social capital explains the interdependencies people develop to be effective in their jobs.

As the diagram below shows, social capital turbocharges human capital. Taken together, human capital + social capital = employee value. Employee value affects the culture, productivity, and performance of the organization and increases the satisfaction and engagement of the employees. In all, it affects retention, customer satisfaction, competitive advantage, sales, revenue, branding, and much more.

The Importance of Social Capital

Human Capital		Social Capital		Employee Value
Explicit Knowledge, Experience, Skills	+	Tacit Knowledge, Trust, Communication, Interdependent relationships	=	Capitalizes on resources Improves performance Affects the culture and engagement

Research indicates that good social capital provides a higher ROI in human capital

Social Capital is diagnosed and measured using Organizational Network Analysis (ONA)

Today, most organizations focus only on the individual—the human capital:

- What can they do?
- What skills do they have?
- What experiences have they had to demonstrate that they can do the job?

Their human capital is important to know in order to measure their competency and place them in the right role. It is often how employees are measured in their job performance reviews—how they contribute as an individual. The interesting part of performance reviews is that employees are often also expected to work in teams.

Yet incentives and how employees are rated on reviews is an individual rank/score. Some companies are changing that but there are still many ratings measured on a curve.

From day one on the job, employees begin to form work relationships. It is natural to want to have relationships and a sense of belonging. Relationships are critical to job satisfaction and growth potential. People need relationships to actualize their skills and ability to have peak performance and productivity.

Belonging supports their need for job and culture fit, which affects retention. At work, it is often easier to get your job done if you like those you work with so you can share information or ask questions to gain more knowledge and experience.

Maybe you have some new ideas or suggestions to make your job easier. Maybe it is an innovation that would help support a product or develop a service for the organization. The performance measures used today miss the fact that work relationships help the individual perform well and that their success is not a solo act.

Social capital has been happening all along since people working together isn't new. Perhaps it is taken for granted. Social capital is not recognized or understood objectively. Yet, it is significant to the effectiveness of the organization. Now we can visualize it and measure it with ONA.

You can't manage what you don't know about or can't measure in some way. With ONA, we can "manage" and utilize the power of social capital to create the culture, environment, or organization that we want while retaining people. Social capital adds value to employees' contributions in the workplace, which enhances the overall organization's effectiveness.

How Do I Know if ONA Is for Me

To find out if ONA is for you, ask yourself these organization-related questions:

- Is your organization getting value out of everyone that is part of it?
- Does your organization effectively capitalize on the employee resources in the organization as a whole?
- Are there challenges or roadblocks to get good ideas implemented?
- Do you have organizational challenges that you aren't sure how to identify or make them tangible so they can be addressed effectively?
- Do you know how to repair your organization when there are challenges or setbacks?

Ask yourself these people-related questions:

- Does your leader know who the people are in the organization that are really doing the work or who are the most important resources for key information, knowledge, projects, and how the work is really done?
- Are there key people in the organization that are overlooked because they don't showcase their contributions but are collaborative and supportive of others they work with?
- Do you have others you work with that are innovative and discuss product enhancements or services but have no way to get them recognized?
- Are most people-decisions made using subjective information?
- When there are major change initiatives, do you know who the change agents really are that will help you succeed? Do you know who might stand in your way?

- Do you have an objective way to identify emerging leaders you might not yet know exist?
- Do you know who is affecting your culture and who lives the values you have for your organization?

These are only a few questions to help you decide if ONA is for you. There are more included in the next section that relate directly to the types of challenges you might encounter.

What Problems Can ONA address?

Common Uses for ONA

There are many applications or use cases for ONA. Here is a list of some possibilities.

Succession planning	Collaboration
Increasing employee engagement	Workplace planning
Organizational change management	Knowledge transfer/ succession
Leveraging diversity	Mergers and acquisitions
Strategic coaching	Multiple generations
Onboarding	Leveraging innovation
Communication	Retention
Talent Management	Optimizing restructuring
Mentoring	Turnover repair
Diversity, Equity, Inclusion (DEI)	Organizational design (physical layout and functional)

To be a bit more focused, here are six applications where ONA is used extensively. I include most of these with examples later in the book. The key business challenges that ONA addresses include talent management, organizational change management, culture, innovation, communication, and mergers and acquisitions. There are subsets of challenges within each of these as well.

Here are some advantages to be gained, and some questions to be addressed that can be answered using ONA for each of these six business challenges.

Talent Management

> The potential for ONA related to talent management is to reduce turnover, improve leadership development, improve succession plans, provide career interest insight, improve and develop employee engagement, improve knowledge transfer, and identify true HIPOs (High Potentials) by combining social capital with human capital analysis.

> The value from using ONA can include training and rehire savings, improved business outcomes/decisions, improved competitive advantage, and increased retention and employee engagement.

Here are some questions that can be addressed when the ONA objective is related to talent management:

- Which employees are most at risk of burnout?
- Where will attrition put us most at risk of losing knowledge and connections?
- How can we reduce the time-to-productivity of new hires?
- What are the behaviors of our high-performing people/teams?
- Who are the real HIPOs?

- What can we do to improve knowledge transfer opportunities?
  Are the leaders actively engaged in the organization or isolated?

Organizational Change Management

➢ The potential for ONA related to organizational change management is to identify real change agents that will help the change succeed (or alternatively who could stand in the way of success), reduce risk and resistance, improve communication during change, and identify roadblocks related to the change.

➢ The value from using ONA can include protecting investments, ensuring the budget and timeline are met for the change, gaining acceptance earlier while reducing risk, reducing the overhead and pain of structural changes, and creating a baseline to measure changes we make.

Here are some questions addressed when the ONA objective is related to organizational change management:

- Who are the influential players/teams (positive or negative) for driving change?
- How do we measure the changes we make?
- Who are the real change agents?
- Who are the key communicators for change?
- Where are the roadblocks to successful change?
- Did the changes we made have an impact?
  If we move people around, what is the impact to the organization/department/workgroup/project?

Culture

> The potential for ONA related to culture is to identify the current culture at a high level, identify the culture carriers, transform an existing culture, combine cultures, or identify the DEI opportunities and progress of an organization—different from the HR statistics and quota objectives.
> The value from using ONA can include an aligned culture, increased customer satisfaction and employee engagement, an improved competitive advantage, and a method to objectively understand if diversity is translating to inclusion that is sustaining.

Here are some questions addressed when the ONA objective is related to culture:

- How do we preserve the culture?
- Which teams/departments/projects are diversified?
- Which teams are roadblocks or bridges?
- Who is disconnected/isolated and why?
  Do we have an inclusive culture?
- Are we aligned to support our vision/mission/values?

Innovation

> The potential for ONA related to innovation is to increase creativity, remove obstacles to innovation, and identify informal innovators—perhaps the real innovators for a company and their organization.
> The value from using ONA can include increased productivity, improved competitive advantage, and reduced one-offs for product/service development for customers.

Here are some questions addressed when the ONA objective is related to innovation:

- How can we stimulate innovation within the organization?
- How can we understand if innovation is occurring?
- How do we know if people are innovating?
- Which people can make a successful team of innovators? Are creative/innovative ideas listened to/implemented? Do we have an 'improvement' culture?

Communication/Collaboration

- ➤ The potential for ONA is to improve communication, collaboration, knowledge sharing, information flow, workflow, planning, and strategy.
- ➤ The value from using ONA can include improved communication and culture, increased trust and productivity, improved engagement/commitment, and improved organization effectiveness.

Here are some questions addressed when the ONA objective is related to communication and/or collaboration:

- How does the work really get done?
- Who helps communication/collaboration across the organization or within departments/groups?
- How do we measure if our project teams are collaborating?
- Where are the communication/collaboration gaps in our organization?
- Who are the key influential employees?
- Who are the employees that are most aware of what is going on across the organization?
- Where are the opportunities to increase communication, collaboration, knowledge sharing, and information flow in the organization?

Mergers and Acquisitions

- ➤ The potential for ONA to support a merger or acquisition is to improve the 60–80% failure rate. M&A initiatives fail largely due to integration issues that are created from combining two distinct cultures and organization structures.
- ➤ The value from using ONA can include reducing the potential loss of revenue that often occurs during transitions, protecting investments, reducing integration costs and improving integration processes and deadlines, providing a roadmap of how best to combine the cultures to reduce risk, and meeting the budget and timeline.

Here are some questions addressed when the ONA objective is related to mergers and acquisitions:

- How can we reduce the failure rate of M&A projects?
- What can we do to improve due diligence for people impact?
- How can we reduce integration issues and costs?
- How can we measure the impact of reducing the workforce?
- How can we measure the impact of restructuring?
- How can we integrate different cultures effectively?
- How can we protect our investment and meet our projections for improved customer satisfaction, competitive advantage, and market share?

Use ONA to "see" how the work is really done, identify leverage points and challenges, and take action that sticks. You need ONA if:

- You find you are having challenges integrating teams, departments, or companies
- You have a major change planned in your organization

- You only address challenges based on symptoms and rarely solve problems or find the cause
- You struggle connecting the dots between business objectives and cultural influences
- You want to improve employee engagement and/or retention
- You face communication/collaboration issues in your organization
- You have silos in your organization and struggle with gaining a competitive advantage
- You think the information and knowledge sharing follows the organization chart
- You don't have a way to understand how soft skills like communication or trust impact the organization
- You need some leverage points to increase productivity and performance to meet business objectives
- You are working toward improved Diversity Equity and Inclusion (DEI) and would like a way to understand if and where it is working or not
- There is misalignment among leaders or across the organization

These are only some of the reasons, and you will uncover more when you read the stories about organizations that follow in the next chapters.

What is ONA?

ONA analyzes, measures, and evaluates the networks that people form in the workplace. ONA produces explicit displays of these networks, which are graphs that look like spider maps. Each component that creates the map has a purpose and meaning.

The components of ONA include nodes, links, directed or undirected connections, graphs/maps of results, and individual networks that represent a topic (e.g., Innovation Network) that an organization is interested in learning more about or that represents key interactions that people have in the workplace (e.g. Work Network).

What is a Network?

When you examine a network, you will hear/read these terms:

- Node – sometimes referred to as *actors*. For the examples throughout the book, the nodes are individual employees for the organization. I sometimes also include customers, projects, departments, vendors, locations, and business units as nodes needed in ONA projects to meet the objective, if required.
- Links – sometimes referred to as edges, lines, connections. A link connects nodes that have an identified relationship.
- Directed connection – when the connection between two nodes is one-way. For example, A to B.
- Undirected connection – when the connection between nodes is two-way. For example, A to B and B to A.
- Graph/map – the visual display of nodes and links that make up a network.
- Network – consists of multiple nodes that are linked in some way based on the reason and value for their connection. Value is usually determined by the frequency/ strength of the connection.

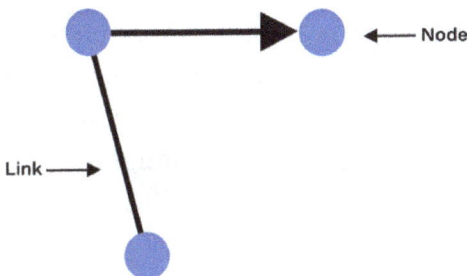

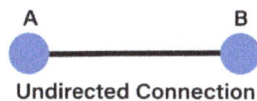

Node

Link

A   B
Directed Connection

A   B
Undirected Connection

Nodes can be inanimate objects, such as computers, buildings, and geographical locations. There needs to be a reason for the connection that is based on a relationship or characteristics they share. These types of inanimate connections do have a relationship, but it is not based on trust.

Trust is a human characteristic. When the type of connection and personal value of the relationship is important to understand while doing ONA, then the nodes are people or some type of node that represents groups of people (e.g., teams, departments).

A two-way connection (undirected) means that person A reports they work with person B and person B reports they work with person A. That is a reciprocal relationship. A one-way connection (directed) means that person A reports they work with person B, but person B doesn't report they work with person A. For a directed link, there is usually an arrow displayed to show the direction of the connection—in this case, person A to person B.

There are many networks in an organization. Some of them include Work, Social, Decision-Making, Expertise, Innovation, Advice, Strategy, Improvement, Career, Problem Solving, Learning, or others that are defined depending on the purpose you have for the ONA.

ONA questions are developed to support the objective for a project and based on the networks included. I refer to some of these networks and what they mean in the stories in Part 2. ONA questions are used in a survey to collect the data needed for software to create the maps and calculate the metrics.

Trust

I mentioned the importance of trust in the leadership lessons I learned. Leaders are looked upon to develop and demonstrate how they trust others and how they can be trusted as leaders. Trust takes time to develop, can be easily broken, and is then difficult to repair.

Leaders must first demonstrate and extend trust to gain acceptance, support, and influence. They must nurture trust to maintain employees who believe them, believe in them, and want to follow them. There are two types of trust in the workplace: task trust and relationship trust.

- Task trust is related to the role of a leader rather than who the leader is as a person. Such things as ability, credibility, consistency, accountability, doing what they say they will do, and ethics are examples of task trust behaviors. In some cases, task trust might be necessary for relationship trust to develop.
- Relationship trust is about a personal connection and is based on attributes such as honesty, caring, compassion, integrity, character, not being self-serving, and being good at listening. Relationship trust is harder to learn and earn or change/develop than task trust.
- Relationship trust is influenced by personality and values. For leaders, relationship trust offers insights into their motives. The leader's behavior is recognized as personally chosen rather than stipulated by a defined role as leader. The leaders' behaviors meet a legitimate need of the employee and can demonstrate an interpersonal concern.

Knowing who you are as a leader in relation to trust is critical to your effectiveness. Trust is vital to engaging employees and retaining talent. Take the time to evaluate trust for yourself and for individuals that you interact with as a leader. Trust is important to create an effective organization. At a high level, trust appears in networks measured by ONA.

For example, an Advice Network displays people that others go to for something personal to them, such as career advice or development advice. That takes more trust in the individual than asking them for a signature on a form or checking to see if their task is complete before you can finish yours. The Work Network, on the other hand, measures task or transactional interactions and is a baseline of organizational knowledge.

Connections in some networks can be purely transactional and not require relationship trust to exist. Those connections might be based on task trust, meaning "I have a task to complete for this project and I know that Barb can help so I will ask her for something to complete the task." Barb might be the subject-matter expert for that task. You might not work with Barb that closely or often, but for some tasks, she is the obvious connection.

For example, maybe it is a procedure that requires Barb's signature for authorization. The person asking for the signature might not know Barb that well. They contact Barb for the signature, explain why they need it, and complete the process. This might occur daily, weekly, or more infrequently.

> *The goal is not to increase the number of connections people have in the networks but to improve their connections and the function of the network itself to gain effectiveness.*

How Does ONA Work?

Active ONA

ONA primarily uses two methods for data collection and analysis, Active ONA and/or Passive ONA. Active ONA uses a survey to gather the data directly from employees or participants. The survey is usually accessed online. If the number of participants is small enough, the survey might be completed through interviews, observations, or paper and pencil type surveys to collect the data.

The participants answer specially designed ONA network questions that ask about work relationships according to topics such as strategy, expertise, work, innovation, and many others. The questions are designed according to the objective you expect or want to find from doing an ONA. The topics create a network that is analyzed based on that topic and its purpose.

The network questions are designed to ask each participant about who they interact with at work based on the topic, and how frequently they do so. The frequency response provides the strength/value of the relationship. Examples of different types of network questions are included in the stories in Part 2 and ONA implementation in Part 3.

Some ONA consultants and vendors might use different methods or questions than I explain in this book. My descriptions include how I do the process and do not cover all the different methods that others use. Active ONA is my preferred method since it can evaluate the personal value of the relationship.

Based on the answers to the ONA survey questions and who picks whom in each question, the software calculates the results and displays the graphical representation of all the links and nodes. The map and metrics report the connections people choose following some algorithms to produce the different strengths, connections, and paths to other individuals in the network.

The goal is not necessarily to increase the number of connections people have in the networks, but to improve their connections and the function of the network itself to gain effectiveness. More connections might be necessary for some but it depends on the context. ONA unlocks and leverages the hidden web of dynamic relationships—the people networks—that form naturally and influence the culture, performance, and growth of the organization.

Passive ONA

Passive ONA is a method to collect data/connections that doesn't require the participants to be involved. Essentially, it is data mining to find patterns and relationships in large amounts of data. Examples of data sources include email data, communication message data from collaboration platforms like Slack, or other relational data like databases and spreadsheets.

Passive ONA is becoming popular, probably because it doesn't require a survey and employee response. I consider it a connect-the-dots version of ONA since there isn't a clear method to understand the strength of the relationship.

For example, assumptions are used to determine the strength of the relationship based on the frequency of messages/communication between the people involved. There are too many variables involved to assume that someone sending ten messages to one person and five to another means that the ten messages imply a more trusted relationship. This becomes more complicated if the data is collected at a particular point in time.

For example, if there is a heated situation or crisis of some type, there are often email messages flying back and forth that might not normally occur, or from which you can't confidently say that the two people exchanging messages want to work together. They are just trying to get through the problem and might not know each other very well. Passive ONA does not capture the content of the messages, so there is no way to know the qualitative value of the connection.

Passive ONA is more of a measure of task relationships for any given topic. However, there is some value to using passive ONA. Passive ONA can be set up to collect data on a regular basis and look for changes more frequently than can be accomplished using a survey and live participants. It also doesn't require the employees to take the time out of their day to respond to a survey.

There is likely good analysis and information to be gained from the data collected, but I see many caveats. I am not opposed to doing this type of ONA. I think it has a place for some objectives. I think results are more effective and richer when they come from the people involved and help to explain the relationships, trust, and interactions in different contexts and situations. Those situations are evaluated within the different network types like Work, Expertise, and Improvement.

Active ONA allows for more nuance and discussion as well as the ability to make organizational decisions more confidently. You get a systems view of the organization and find data specific to the purpose. For example, if you want to evaluate if an organization is aligned and shares business strategy across multiple departments or companies, Active ONA is much easier to analyze.

Data from email or communication platforms might provide discussion points about strategy but likely don't include the core relationships involved in strategy information flow and participation. Typically, those discussions occur in meetings since they often involve perspectives from many different individuals and in-depth discussions with nuance to negotiate or build consensus to move forward.

I do see value in combining the two methods since email or other available relationship data could provide some detail or validate the connections reported through the survey collection. However, that might be an added expense you don't want.

> *The intuition you have about people you work with, work for, or who work for you can be validated or explained visually and in detail using ONA.*

Why ONA is a "Have to Have"

I believe in ONA so much that I continue to find ways to get beyond the cool factor alone. I strive to get more leaders and decision makers to understand the value of using ONA to get a clear understanding of how the work is really happening in their organization.

This book shares experiences of organizations using ONA and couples it with other services or actions to offer solutions for you to learn about. The examples will help you understand how the intuition you have about people you work with, work for, or who work for you can be validated or explained visually and in detail using ONA.

You will "see" the organization and the people that work there in a different and meaningful way. ONA provides insight, perspective, and information for you as a leader, employee, decision maker, or perhaps just someone who is interested in your organization and wants the people to be more effective and productive.

I chose key client experiences I have supported using ONA over the years. Some of the ideas and issues shared in the examples might be something you are experiencing as well.

Influential Factors

There are some influential factors that are important in terms of ONA. These factors have evolved and are part of the fabric of organizations that might have pushed ONA forward a bit more quickly towards acceptance by and awareness of decision makers.

> *Leaders are aware of the hierarchy and intuitively know that people interact with others in the workplace. They aren't aware of the power and complexity of the emerging networks and the impact the people networks have in the organization. ONA provides awareness.*

Perhaps the following factors will offer some reasons to consider using ONA for your organization. It is this confluence of factors and how they dynamically relate that affects leadership decisions, management styles, and the changing workplace. The factors are Technology, Globalization, and Generations. I will touch on these factors briefly. I have experienced these factors working with clients. They can be diagnosed using ONA. You will learn more about them in the stories.

These factors are also mentioned in O'Hara Devereaux's book, *Navigating the Badlands: Thriving in the Decade of Radical Transformation*, published in 2004. Her book compelled me over the years to consider these terms as they relate to ONA and the leadership paradigm shift that she explains. She believed that the leadership shift must take place for leaders to adapt, understand, and lead change, and to be flexible.

The leadership paradigm shift has been going on for some time. Some leaders don't seem aware of it, but those that are face challenges. They are creating change. A shift doesn't mean throwing things out completely or starting over. It means there are some alterations or tweaks that eventually create change.

In the case of ONA, it means leaders should learn about the social capital in their organization. It will help them with the leadership paradigm shift they are facing and is inevitable. Leaders need to understand the impact it has on their success and that of the organization to meet the business objectives.

Leadership Paradigm Shift

Organizations are dynamic because people are involved and because change happens. Management and leaders in organizations need to be flexible and responsive to change. Yet, the methods that leaders use to make decisions remain largely subjective as they relate to the people decisions and organizational change.

Management styles that have been used over the years have been somewhat stagnant and have become stale. They do not meet the needs of a dynamic organization. Maybe relying on these tired styles has made leaders inflexible and caused them to struggle with their response to change.

The diagram here indicates that organizations have both a hierarchy (org chart) and a *shadow or emerging* people network. There can be balance and they do coexist in organizations. Perhaps one business objective requires more hierarchical influence and another, like organizational change, requires more network influence.

Leaders who grasp and utilize both are making the paradigm shift to a better workplace and improved organizations. Either way, both are present and participating. It is a matter of how aware of each a leader might be and what they do about it.

Most leaders are fully aware of the hierarchy. It is usually captured in a form like the diagram below. Leaders also intuitively know that people interact with others in the workplace. They aren't aware of the power and complexity of the emerging network and the impact it has on the organization. ONA provides awareness and turns their intuition into science.

Formal & Emerging Organization Structures

ONA provides a new lens to evaluate how people show up in an organization

Compatible, not mutually exclusive

Hierarchy
- Explicit visibility
- Rigid
- Uses rules for knowledge
- Transactional relationship
- Slow change

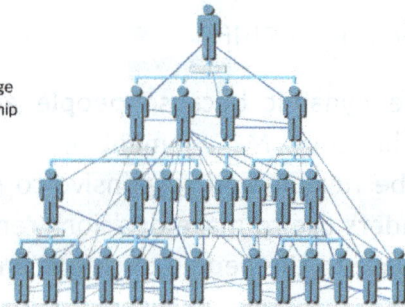

Network
- Tacit visibility
- Flexible
- Uses ties for knowledge
- Trust relationship
- Rapid, radical change

© All Rights Reserved Selfy, Inc.

The hierarchy is commonly known and expressed explicitly through the organization chart. The emerging network, whether it is known to leaders or not, is not commonly expressed explicitly.

ONA makes it explicit and manageable. Yet, ONA is still relatively unknown.

Gartner research classified the reach of Social Network Analysis (SNA) around 2007 as "adolescent," meaning having between 5 and 20% market penetration and being relatively new to the marketplace. At the 20% higher end, the report included companies that use it as a backend process for data mining and to begin developing algorithms in response. These companies wanted to understand relationships between consumer responses and products/services they offer.

Examples of those who adopted SNA earlier might be marketing companies or government agencies. SNA is used heavily for law enforcement, the military, and in the hard sciences, such as for tracking viruses. So, it has been used and available for many years in other disciplines. For use in business organizations, it is still unique.

There is a leadership paradigm shift occurring, even if it isn't moving as quickly as some would like. The point that matters, for this book, is that we haven't made a lot of progress improving management styles even though the workplace has changed and continues to change.

There isn't one style that fits every organization nor a perfect style for every leader. The demands from employees and the three influential factors I mentioned are making a big difference and creating a slow but progressing change—a leadership paradigm shift.

Factors Related to the Leadership Paradigm Shift

Technology, Generational influences, and Globalization are demanding changes in management and leadership styles and methods. These factors are not new concepts but there is a lot of change among them. Taken together, and considering how they dynamically interact, requires us to place more emphasis on the changes needed to understand and manage the workplace differently and effectively today.

Organizations and leaders do recognize and "feel" the need for change. They experience these factors but might not have a way to grasp and discern how they affect their organization. I often hear leaders talk about them as an annoyance or challenge. They scratch their heads about what to do about them. However, the impact is one we cannot ignore.

The presence of the factors and the dynamics they create makes ONA important as a tool to come to terms with and grasp how these factors affect your organization. Generational and globalization influences can be measured directly using ONA. You will see some of that with the stories and cases coming in the next section of the book.

Technology is a catalyst to information and knowledge sharing, collaboration, and communication paths—other factors that ONA measures. All these factors involve people. ONA makes their impact explicit and reports to you how the workplace is affected.

Power Networks

Another aspect that O'Hara Devereaux emphasized about ONA is that people networks are power networks. Her definition of a strategic power network is one that you can design to support a specific initiative. Leaders can use the influential web of relationships and build on those to support the initiative and manage it to success.

> *People Networks are Power Networks and can make or break your strategic goals and tactical plans. They can stand in the way of change or be the first adopters of it.*

Devereaux points out that not using ONA is no longer viable. It creates maps of explicit networks and what is really happening to affect projects, initiatives, or just everyday interactions in the workplace. She emphasized that ONA is a way to understand your organization and how power networks affect it.

Devereaux states that you don't have the option of ignoring the networks in your organization any longer. She suggests three specific actions for using the networks:

- Map the networks
- Identify key people and their connections
- Optimize and align them with strategic goals

Devereaux emphasized that ONA is a critical success factor in improving business objectives and strategy. She also recognized that any powerful tool can be misused. However, leaders that use networks to make decisions and enhance their leadership will identify and drive manipulative leaders from power more effectively than merely hierarchical organizations can. I emphasize to my clients that ONA is not to be used for punitive purposes.

Devereaux understood it is key for organizations to interconnect across the organization, generations, or cultural boundaries. She pointed out that power networks can make or break your strategic goals and tactical plans. They can stand in the way of change or be the first adopters of it.

Networks hold the culture carriers of your organization. It is critical that you identify them along with the key influencers, the change agents, and the emerging leaders as only ONA can do for you. Yes, you might have some ideas of who these key people are. That is your intuition. You might be right, and you might be wrong. The only way to know for sure is to take the time to use ONA and turn your intuition into science.

Identify the Leadership Paradigm Shift

Companies are recognizing issues in terms of performance management, retention, recruitment, employee engagement/satisfaction, recognition, and career development. These are certainly important indicators of organizational health, but they are symptoms or outcomes.

The symptoms indicate that you haven't really fixed or stabilized the problem. The problems might have been going on for years and are likely indicators of the leadership paradigm shift, or are calling out for the shift to happen.

Globalization

Globalization brought more diversity and change to the workplace. Companies moved resources from their home bases or built their companies in other countries to expand their revenue and brand and create more innovation and competition. Companies used new options to find employees and welcome employees from other countries. They were primarily looking to reduce costs and in the process, found a lot of change introduced that affected business decisions.

Globalization affects how a company communicates, operates, and defines its culture. In fact, culture as a term is usually associated with a particular country's culture in this context. Environment is a more general term to allow for reference to country-specific cultural differences but still reference a common workplace environment that includes company norms and values.

> *ONA is especially useful for leaders who are virtual from the workforce, in multiple countries or locations, or in today's remote and work from home options.*

Does the country of origin, or the business owner, define the country-culture that dominates a workplace? If so, how do the people who are not citizens of the country of origin, who have a different country-culture, adapt or feel included? Are they accepted? Can they communicate effectively? Do employees representing multiple cultures integrate effectively to do their work together? ONA answers these questions and more.

ONA provides a method to identify, analyze, and track objectively how globalization is affecting a department, group, organization, or entire company. It is an especially useful tool for leaders who are virtual from the workforce, in multiple countries or locations, or in today's remote and work from home options.

- How else can they possibly have objective data from all these different locations at the same time?
- How can they really know how the work is getting done?
- Is there a consistent/equitable workplace environment in each location?
- What can leaders rely on to understand employees from different locations and know if, how, and who they interact with to make an impact on the organization?
- What does that impact look like?

ONA closes the gaps and offers valuable insight to leaders who might not be physically around most employees.

Communication for a Global Company

Here is an example of a global technology company using ONA for a communication issue. My contact was the SVP of Engineering who led the growth and strategy of the data communication network. The data network supported the technology that their company developed and provided for their customers.

The SVP was one of the engineers that worked for me at the last technology start-up that I led before starting my consulting business. So, the trusted relationship that I developed years ago was still intact. He asked me to meet with him so he could describe the issue they were having but couldn't seem to solve.

He explained, "We have a company that has grown quickly and substantially. We have two large primary groups, sales, and engineering. Our company maintains an entrepreneurial mindset with the founders of the company as part of our executive leadership. Our company has offices in seven different countries so communication can be a challenge."

He continued with the background and then got to the core of the problem. "With the economy down right now, our sales team is pushing hard to get products developed when customers ask for them. We have a communication problem between sales and engineering. We tried to get it resolved before bringing you here today."

He continued, "We hired two different consulting companies to sort it out. One provided communication training, which wasn't what we needed. The other one spent three days facilitating a combined session of the sales and engineering leaders in a room together for hours at a time. All we ended up with was finger-pointing and no solution. All at a significant expense to bring global leaders together for those three days."

He asked me what I could do. I explained that if it was ultimately a communication issue of some type, it would be visible from the results of the ONA survey. The results would also offer him a broader perspective of how the organization interacts, especially since they were so geographically dispersed.

If the problem was communication as they defined it, ONA would visibly identify which countries were most affected, who was involved or not involved to help solve the problem, and who could close the gaps and find solutions.

He agreed to move forward. I completed the ONA analysis and went over the initial results. He said, "I think you found the real problem and when you present it to the management team, make sure you point out what you shared with me. I think they will like this."

When I returned later to present the findings, the room was packed with all the executives, the founders, and other key management. I had a map that I thought described the core problem explicitly (see Map A).

I explained, "Communication flows primarily within the sales group and within the engineering group. However, to get the customer requirements to a point where a product is developed, communication must be shared between sales and engineering using some type of procedure or process. There is a very small group of five people who are responsible for product development." They were the process.

> *Once they saw Map A, the director of the product development group stood up and introduced himself. He proudly stated, "I am a bottleneck."*

I continued, "My experience with product development tells me that a functional team takes the customer requirements from the salespeople. There is some type of review process to decide if it is cost effective to develop a product and if it will help more than one customer.

"Then they put it in a form for engineering to design and develop the product. This group is responsible for sending it to the engineering group to prioritize and begin development. The product team has the knowledge of all customer requirements, different sales requests, and the stages of product development for approved products."

They agreed this was the intent and process they had defined. Once they saw Map A, the director of the product development group stood up and introduced himself. He proudly stated, "I am a bottleneck." The room laughed and I said, "You aren't wrong, and here is why."

I explained that his small group of five product development personnel had the responsibility of a well-designed process. "My understanding is that the current economic conditions are making it tough for salespeople to make their quotas. They are working with customers to come up with products they will buy."

I continued, "The salespeople are going directly to engineers to convince them to develop a customer requested product as a one-off and to get it to that customer quickly. They don't want to work with the product development group because they might not agree to accept the request. If they do, it takes too long before it is ready for the customer."

I explained the impact that, "This bypasses the process, causes confusion, frustration, and increases costs overall. Not to mention, it is delaying other product development and confusing the engineers about what gets priority and who they should respond to."

They all agreed this was what was happening. They framed it as a "communication problem" since there were so many different requests from different parts of the world, and they were indeed avoiding the product development group. No one had put it all together for everyone to understand the part they played in causing the issue. ONA made it clear.

Although it is not obvious from Map A that Globalization played a part, it did. The sales employees were from seven different countries and going directly to the engineers. It made the problem more complex to figure out since there were so many different people involved who weren't coordinating their requests and they were competing for results.

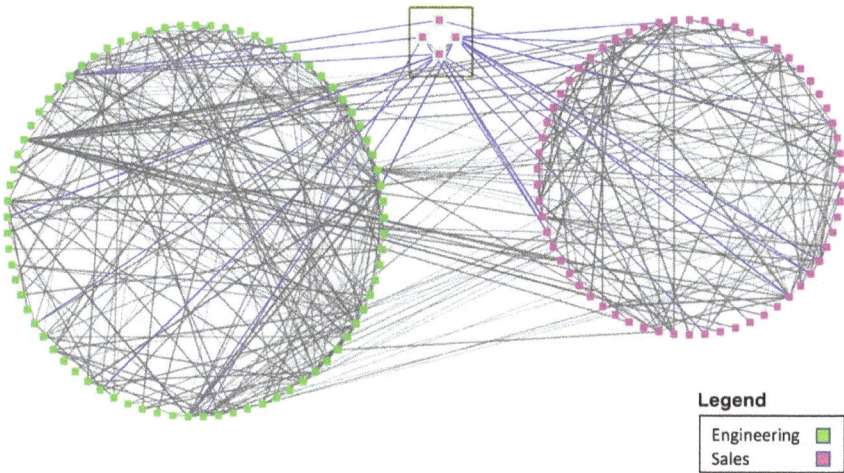

Map A. Innovation Network. The four pink nodes in the box are the product development team. One pink node is missing from the box as that person did not have a two-way connection with either group. The gray lines are within and between the two groups and indicate product requests or discussions. The blue lines show there are a few that do follow the process. Most of the interaction is directly between sales and engineering, rather than product development.

Map A doesn't distinguish country location but that could be another way to look at the problem and pinpoint which locations were ignoring the process. That additional information could be helpful to find out more about why they went around the process and get suggestions to fine tune it, not for finger-pointing. That is an example of a follow-up exercise to learn more details and context about the situation.

> *What they thought was a communication problem was causing a management nightmare. The process they had developed was bypassed. It affected the attitudes and productivity of the employees.*

Other Issues

What they thought was a communication problem was causing a management nightmare. It affected the attitudes and productivity of the employees. The other consultants were not able to resolve the issues because they didn't know the core problem and didn't address it from the systems perspective that ONA offers.

It was undeniable when you could see it visualized and understand the procedure they developed wasn't necessarily broken. The process was bypassed for different reasons. One was that the product development team was only five people. Three of them were in management. That might have explained why the salespeople were frustrated.

It added to the wait time that there were few resources that were doing the work. In the meeting, the CEO immediately said to the director of product development, "I want you to double your group immediately and work to resolve this issue—it is your priority!"

There were other maps as well with valuable information. The Work Network was unusually busy with a lot of communication and information flows. I commented, "There is an unusual amount of frequent communication for the number of people involved, even though this is the busiest network for any organization."

When I said that, the CEO stopped me and said, "I thought communication was a good thing." I agreed but explained, "There are different types of communication. More isn't necessarily better." This is where context is important to the analysis and to grasp what is happening in an organization.

So, I went further and pointed to some patterns in the map. I said, "This degree of communication might indicate:

- That people must spend a lot of their day interacting because they don't have training and confidence to complete a task

- They don't have a process to follow
- They aren't sure who they are supposed to work with or what the priorities are supposed to be
- Or because of the core issue we just uncovered, they are unsure they should be doing something and want to check to avoid retribution."

This problem was obviously causing a lot of grief with management and perhaps the lower levels were feeling some stress from it. They acted immediately in several ways.

1. They doubled the Product Development group with more non-management employees.
2. They restructured the organization and eliminated a layer of management to streamline communication and workflow.
3. They revisited their training programs, especially for new employees.
4. They reviewed their processes and procedures.
5. They spoke to individuals directly affected to see how or what they needed for support or changes.
6. They interviewed the sales, engineering, and product development people for ideas to improve the product development process.

Later, I met with the SVP again. He was pleased with the results, interaction in the meeting, and the enlightenment of the management team. They were happy to have answers and ideas of what was really happening. He quizzed me further on some comments I made about the over communication indicators and other implications for his organization.

> *I used an example of one of the key influencers that*
> *I uncovered from the results. It is a common occurrence that*
> *the best people are overloaded. I showed the SVP the*
> *patterns around this individual and that it could mean*
> *he was close to burnout.*

I used an example of one of the key influencers that I uncovered from the results. As it turned out, he was a key engineer with a lot of experience. He was the go-to person for problem solving, expertise, project involvement and much more.

It is a common occurrence that the best people are overloaded. I showed the SVP the patterns around this individual and that it could mean he was close to burnout. If he didn't want this person to resign or experience burnout, he might have to make some changes.

He said, "I am going to meet with him and see what he thinks. I think he will tell me if he is getting too many requests and distractions." He met with the individual. That person admitted that he was overworked, and he was exhausted from all the requests and trying to support others that weren't sure what to do.

The SVP made changes in the workflow and demands to avoid losing this employee. He also reviewed the onboarding and training process for his department. The SVP told me he was going to incorporate social capital information in the performance management process for his department and work with HR to consider it for the company.

Technology

Another of the three factors is Technology. Technology has shifted over the years from a separate function to an integrated part of everything that happens to operate a business. Technology has supported and perhaps sped up globalization. It made it much easier for people in the same organization but in different parts of the world to stay connected and communicate in some way.

Technology isn't measured directly using ONA. Technology is a catalyst for change, innovation, collaboration and much more. These outcomes can be measured using ONA. There are examples of these outcomes in some of the stories in the following chapters.

Generational Influences

Today there are four to five generations in the workplace; Traditionalists, Baby Boomers, Gen X, Gen Y or millennials, and Gen Z. Millennials are the predominant generation in the workforce at the time of this writing, making up about 35% of the labor force. They are also the upcoming leaders in the organizations.

Millennials have been a big influence on changes in the organization culture, structure, and management styles. In general, they prefer environments that are collaborative, with open communication and diversity. ONA is likely something that millennial decision-makers will quickly understand the value of and see it as a have-to-have. Much like the student that thought it was obvious for leaders to use ONA.

There are examples of generational influences and impact using ONA in some of the following chapter stories.

Synthesis

These key factors—technology, generations, and globalization—come together in the workplace and influence how people interact. What are the outcomes and impact of these influences?

Some outcomes are the leadership paradigm shift, throwing out performance management systems, managers as coaches, gig workers, work environment changes, more relaxed work environments, virtual work options, increased awareness of diversity, equity, and inclusion (DEI), and many others.

Not only are generations and globalization creating change in the workplace, but these factors bring diversity as well. Diversity over time might not require "numbers" to be met or require a specific initiative and focus to achieve. It might become the status quo.

The key factors I highlight do not affect every organization equally, nor do some of the outcomes impact organizations and leaders equally. They touch the business or company in some way regarding their interaction with clients and/or other companies to meet their business objectives. ONA is available to leaders to isolate and focus on some of these factors, like generations, to measure, analyze and enhance the organization further.

> *Missing the opportunity to find leverage points can cause management to spend time on symptoms alone and waste company resources and money.*

ONA can identify where and how these factors are impacting company culture and the organization. It can detect leverage points that might go unnoticed otherwise. Missing the opportunity to find leverage points can cause management to spend time on symptoms alone, waste company resources and money, and never fix the underlying causes. Look back on the communication issues from the technology company between sales and engineering as an example.

Let's look at diversity a little closer. In most cases, HR is concerned about this and provides training to employees. For some, that is as far as it goes. Others might be paying closer attention to having equity in processes or benefits. HR might use the different demographics to fulfill the company objective and make a quota. They likely include these demographics in their metrics related to retention, promotions, and development opportunities.

That is important and is likely tracked for the Key Performance Indicators (KPIs) of the organization. However, the magic of workplace DEI focus should be on the "I," inclusion. Making the numbers doesn't tell you anything about the actual inclusion of those diverse individuals. It isn't just about how many of X you hire, but whether they stay in your organization and become part of the culture.

Inclusion is what tells you if diversity is working or not. ONA is the best method to know for sure if employees are included in the culture, projects, and teams where they are assigned. There are examples of what that looks like in some of the stories that follow. Here are some questions that ONA helps to answer related to DEI.

- Are employees isolated or part of a team/group that is helping them grow in their career?
- Do groups of diverse individuals create silos or cliques because they don't feel like they belong?
- Are they integrated into the groups/teams they are assigned to?
- Do you know how much influence they have on other employees?
- If they are experts in some way, do they share their expertise? Do others go to them for their expertise?
- If I make a change in their work role or team, how will that affect their social capital?

There is more to diversity than common measures related to gender, race, ethnicity, generation, or others that are usually tracked. Many organizations realize that diversity of thought, religion, sexual preference, and others are also important to consider. However, there are many privacy concerns that go with any type of diversity.

ONA can measure any attribute or demographic that is shared in the data collection. I referred to the more common that most people are okay with identifying for data collection purposes.

The questions can also be measured and answered using ONA and you can act if needed. If you think you know the answers based on your intuition, turn intuition into science using ONA to know for sure.

PART TWO:

ONA IN ACTION

2
COMMUNICATION, TRUST, ENGAGEMENT

OVERVIEW

Problem: A year after a major software change, the CIO was not getting the expected results.

Why: The CIO identified a communication problem between two groups. He was experiencing retention issues and employee engagement survey scores that were troublesome.

What: The CIO thought he isolated the problem as a communication issue between two groups. He wanted to have a custom team building workshop for the two groups. We did an ONA first. After the ONA, the root cause was identified as a trust issue among the management team. The CIO validated that this was the issue using the employee engagement results and asked for solutions.

He used his budget to develop employee-led change initiatives to address the six engagement scores that would have the most impact. He also requested a management development program including coaching.

Outcomes:

- Identified trust as the root cause of the issue. Avoided cost of team building workshop.
- Improved engagement scores over two years, resulting in the most improved department in the company.
- Reduced turnover from 17% to under 2%. This saved retraining and rehiring costs of over $3 million.
- Restructured the management team and improved relationships through coaching and management development.

Identified Trust as Root Cause

I had been working with the CIO of a Fortune 10 company for about a year on an organizational change management project. The change had an impact on the IT department of about 70 people who would be getting used to new processes and new roles and responsibilities, as well as the new software and training for their work.

There were two groups out of seven, programmers and systems analysts, that had to work together seamlessly to support their customers. Each had a manager. The CIO came to me after the software change had been implemented for about one year. He thought he noticed some conflict, lack of effective communication, and resistance within these two groups. He thought he had identified the problem and the solution.

He said, "I want you to develop a custom team building workshop. I think we have a communication issue between two of the IT groups." What he was seeing were the symptoms, not the real cause of the problem. This was his intuition working and he was confident he had it figured out. He was a successful and experienced leader.

Since I had been working with the teams and managers directly for about a year, I didn't think this was the problem. I suggested, "Let's find out for sure before putting money into a custom idea that would be costly and perhaps a short-term solution at best. Let's try an Organizational Network Analysis to identify the challenges and leverage points to find out what is really going on." I described the process, and he was willing to try it.

The problem and cause were clear. It was not a communication problem between the two groups (see Map 1), it was a trust issue among the managers (see Map 2). Once I showed the maps to the CIO and pointed out what they meant, he could visibly see that he needed to shift gears. He authorized funds for management development and work with the employees on improvement initiatives to increase engagement.

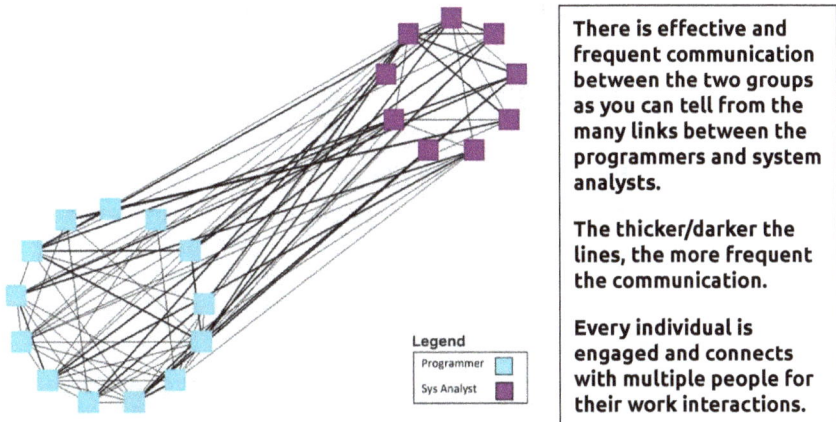

There is effective and frequent communication between the two groups as you can tell from the many links between the programmers and system analysts.

The thicker/darker the lines, the more frequent the communication.

Every individual is engaged and connects with multiple people for their work interactions.

Legend
Programmer
Sys Analyst

Map 1. Work Network. Communication between programmers and system analysts.

Map 2 below indicates that the managers are involved in problem solving. They are hands-on managers. Overall, there is little collaboration in the IT department when there are problems to solve. This could delay getting solutions in a timely manner. It also indicates that knowledge sharing about the problem is limited.

Should the problem occur again, it might be reworked from the start if there are not multiple paths to share the knowledge.

Most of the problem solving goes between two people and then the next one in line. Much like a game of telephone to pass it on. That creates a risk of diluting the solution and problem-solving process. This is one example where more connections would be better.

Among the two groups analyzed regarding communication in Map 1, there is reasonable problem-solving among the programmers and systems analysts. They aren't problem solving only with their own team. Another good sign that they are communicating effectively.

The architecture group tends to solve problems within their own group and with three of the managers. That could be because of escalation procedures. The managers themselves are not effective collaborators while participating in problem solving situations. This indicated trust issues among managers, along with other networks that confirmed the same.

Context helps to explain what some network patterns mean. During the work with the IT department, the CIO was focused on improving the engagement results and management development, so we didn't go deeper with each network. However, that could be done as a follow-on action.

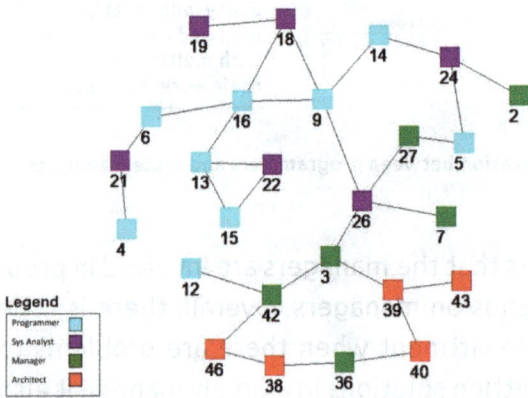

Map 2. Problem Solving Network. The managers in the IT department were not collaborating or sharing information as shown by the few connections between them.

This indicated a trust issue among managers. The trust issue was confirmed with the employee engagement survey results.

Other Data Adds Context for the CIO

In the meantime, the company had just completed their annual corporate-wide employee engagement survey. I didn't know they were doing this while I was collecting the ONA data. When I had the ONA results, I went to the CIO to inform him what I thought the cause of communication concerns might be for the IT department.

I reported that ONA pointed to a problem with trust among the managers. The CIO responded, "You know, you are right!" I laughed because he said it so emphatically and with a look on his face like I had some superpower or something. I wasn't sure where he was going with this, so I said, "I'm glad I am right, but why are you saying that? You haven't seen the results yet."

He said, "We just completed our corporate employee engagement survey. All the indicators out of the twenty categories that measure some type of relationship or communication with your manager/supervisor were the lowest rated." On top of that, there were only two categories out of twenty that were green; the rest were red."

The corporate engagement survey results were measured with red, yellow, or green indicators. The colors are used to compare the entire corporation's results to departments and previous years' results. In this case, the CIO was referring to the IT department results. Green meant the individual department scored higher, yellow meant they were the same, red meant the individual department scored lower.

The CIO was obviously concerned. He knew this reflected not just on him but could also explain what he was already experiencing with much higher turnover than he was used to. Turnover was now at 17%. The ONA results and employee survey results agreed with each other. He had evidence and context for the issues he was facing. It was objective data that he couldn't ignore.

He said, "Okay, you identified the real problem and I have supportive evidence and metrics from the engagement survey. Now I want you to take the engagement survey results and figure out how to improve them." He gave me the engagement survey results for his department. I suggested we take the six engagement areas that were the lowest and/or would have the most impact. We couldn't improve all twenty but these six might help the others too.

> *We developed initiatives around each of the six engagement survey results that would have the most impact. We involved the employees to work on them together.*

We developed initiatives around each of the six and involved the employees to work on them together. I invited the employees to attend focus groups and organizational meetings to get started. They were excited to be involved. The employees did the work and came up with plans and ideas. I facilitated the ongoing organized meetings per initiative topic to keep them moving forward.

I also met with all the managers weekly and worked on different ideas for communication and effective collaboration. We explored the ONA results for the managers to realize and see how they were or were not interacting in the organization and their impact to their respective groups.

Management vs. Individual Contributor

The management development plan was to start building trust among them. In addition, there were individual coaching sessions. They had to think more in terms of "we" and not "I." ONA captures how they interact with their team and peers. It also gives clues to help build or develop relationships.

> *The managers on this team knew they didn't have a balance.*
> *There was confirmation in the ONA results.*

There were seven managers. Map 2 includes only six of the seven managers. The Quality Assurance manager wasn't connected to the other managers at all and in some cases, not even to his own direct reports. It was interesting since there were a lot of complaints about this individual related to his abilities, his communication style, his sense of urgency or lack of response, and ability to collaborate. That was confirmed in the ONA results.

Example Using ONA for Coaching

ONA creates data that can produce a micro-view of teams, groups, projects, or individuals. As part of the management development, I produced *ego networks* for each manager. An ego network is essentially a map that shows the direct connections for an individual in a hub/spoke design (see Map 3). Often the ego network also includes connections two steps out from the individual. For this example, only the direct connections were needed.

One of the six managers was recently promoted because of his strong technical and organizational skills. He was asked by the CIO to clean up the performance and productivity group that responded to outages and problem tickets.

He was a great problem solver, but when he was promoted into this management position, he seemed to depart from his area of competence. However, he thought he was doing great. He cleaned up the department related to processes and response times. The CIO thought he made the right choice when he promoted this individual since efficiency improved.

What neither of them understood was that this manager was upsetting the employees reporting to him and others that had to interact with him or his group. He had created a group who now were so structured and rigid that they were unapproachable. The environment changed from collaboration to strict rules of engagement. Most of his direct reports were seasoned professionals so they didn't appreciate the changes.

The manager was too wrapped up in his own expertise. He had no management experience and thought he could rely on the relationships he had when he was their peer. He didn't notice that others now saw him as their boss and that created a new type of relationship for them. He was telling them what to do rather than having a conversation with them or asking their opinions and tapping into their expertise.

He also didn't realize that along with responsibility and authority, he had created an environment of compliance that he interpreted as trust. People did what they were told. He didn't know that behind his back they were complaining and becoming disengaged.

Using ONA for Coaching

He talked *to* them rather than *with* them, which doesn't work well with knowledge workers especially. Some of them were seasoned technical people who really didn't need to be told what to do. Yet his perspective was they had trusted relationships with him.

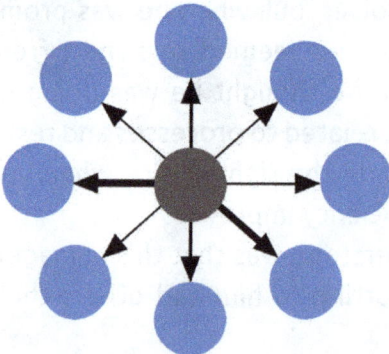

Map 3. The Individual Network (Ego Network) for the manager. This map shows the manager in the middle.

All the connections to people in his group go out from him to his direct reports but there are no reciprocal connections from his direct reports back to him.

It was apparent in the ONA and engagement survey results they didn't trust him. Having interviewed several of his direct reports, I validated the context of the data. When I sat down with him during his coaching session, I showed him the ONA map (See Map 3). I quizzed him about being a trusted leader and he was quick to say, "I talk to my staff regularly, so they trust me." He had a blind spot.

However, because he was a technical professional, it was hard for him to disagree with the data. It came from the people he worked with, but he was surprised to learn this. He recognized that his strength was as an individual contributor, so he opted out as a manager but remained in IT. He just wasn't right for a management role.

This was eye-opening for the CIO, who was a seasoned leader and adept at identifying people to fit a position. In this case, he was blind to the fact that this individual couldn't balance the people-side with the demands of the position. He knew he could technically do the job—and he did.

The CIO just didn't realize he would alienate so many people in the process. Sometimes making the transition from non-management to first line management is the biggest change for people and they may not realize what the expectations of the role are.

Human Capital Impact

Another important outcome from the change initiatives was to improve employee engagement. We measured the score changes over the course of two years. The first year the six categories we selected improved from 9% to 21%. Over the course of two years, the improvement ranged from 19%–32% (see Table A). The turnover rate also dropped from 17% to less than 2%. Both measures stabilized during the CIO's tenure with the company.

ONA contributed to the increase in employee engagement scores and the reduction in turnover. The CIO also changed the management structure. The management development program emphasized how much more the managers needed to share information and work together as a team. They learned to trust, collaborate more, and spend time together to achieve their goals.

Table A. This table identifies the six goal categories selected to improve the employee engagement scores. We designed employee-led change initiatives. The table indicates the percentage increase over two years.

Employee Engagement Goal Category	% Increase
Engagement	19%
Involvement	32%
Supervisor Relations	32%
Work Organization	18%
Goals/Objectives	15%
Training	19%

The following year, the IT department was identified as the most improved in employee engagement scores and they won an award at the corporate level. They were invited to attend the corporate conference to receive the award and entertain questions about how they improved so dramatically and so quickly.

All the red turned green, and they saved over $3 million in turnover and training costs by using the ONA results and focusing on the engagement initiatives. That alone was a big return on investment (ROI) for the CIO. The engagement score increases very likely reflected increased customer satisfaction, employee productivity, and performance as well.

When Someone Leaves the Organization

There was another situation that the ONA results helped to understand and mitigate. One of the key systems analysts (See Map 4a, Node 26) notified the CIO that she would resign. This happened just as I finished the data analysis for the ONA results and before any of the other solutions were developed.

I had a meeting scheduled with the CIO. He said, "I just found out that a systems analyst is leaving. This really impacts our organization as she is a key employee and next in line for succession to management." I asked him who it was and knew the maps would show him some valuable information.

Not only was she a key contributor, but she was also one of the main connectors to bridge the groups in the IT organization. You can see the impact in the maps and the comparison after taking her node out of the network (Map 4b). I remembered seeing how critical node 26 was to their organization.

I said, "I need to show you the ONA maps." I showed him Map 4a and pointed out that she was node 26 and what it meant. His face lost its color. He said, "What should I do now?"

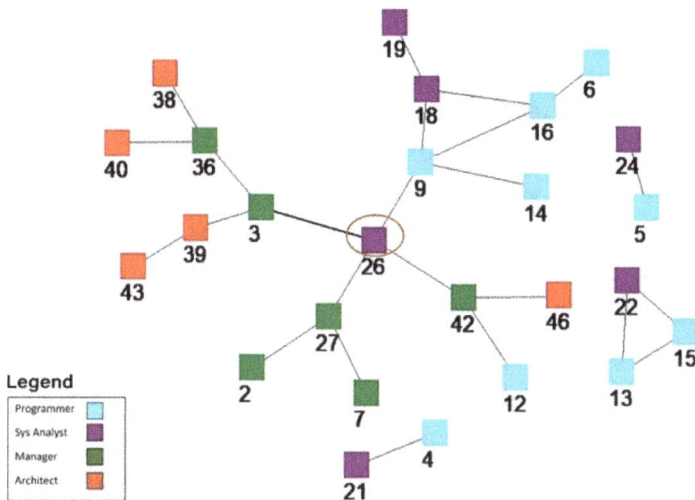

Map 4a. The Work Network with node 26.

Map 4a. The Work Network shows the significance of node 26, circled in red. She was the central bridge to everyone in the core network depicted.

Map 4b. The second view of the Work Network shows the disconnected core network when node 26 leaves the organization. Those she was directly connected to can be identified and brought into the transition plans to mitigate the impact.

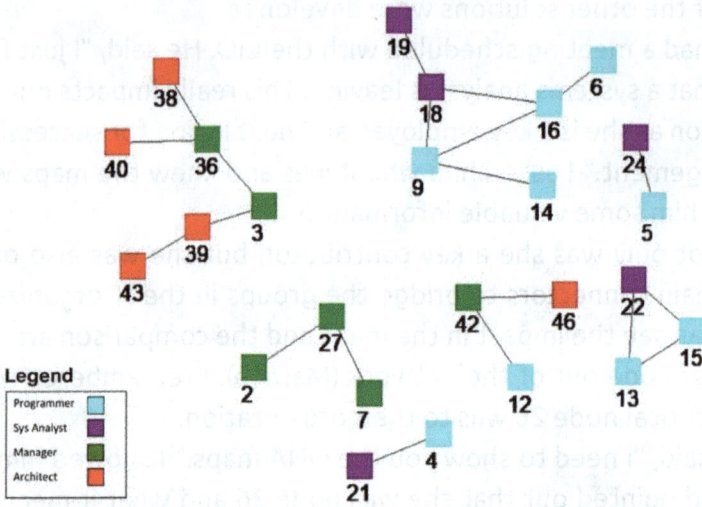

Map 4b. The Work Network with node 26 removed.

I asked him "Is there any chance to retain her?" He said "No." I explained, "You can still use the ONA data to find who she is primarily connected to and start working with them for knowledge transfer. Perhaps you can ask if she would stay a few weeks longer to have more time for her to train and share information with those that will be assigned her workload."

He thought that was a great idea. It helped the remaining employees get up to speed faster and capture some of her knowledge. It also helped her manager while he was finding a replacement.

ONA can be used to mitigate the impact of someone leaving the organization or moving to a different group. ONA provides human capital risk management.

3

ORGANIZATIONAL STRUCTURE, STRATEGY, COMMUNICATION

OVERVIEW

Problem: 1) The executive team was not aligned to support the enterprise strategy. 2) There were communication issues identified in the employee engagement survey results that could affect retention.

Why: The CEO wanted an aligned enterprise strategy that supported their brand, sales, marketing, customer service and satisfaction, and ensured a competitive advantage. He also wanted to address engagement survey results that indicated retention risk related to communication issues.

What: The CEO knew the enterprise structure encouraged silos. He respected the independence of the individual operating companies. He wanted the presidents of each company to recognize the importance of an aligned strategy. So far, he didn't have a method that persuaded them to work together proactively. ONA was the method to get their attention.

Outcome: The Strategy Network was explicit and revealed the issue. The enterprise communication analysis identified key trusted communicators the CEO could meet with to enhance communication in response to the engagement survey results.

- ONA gave the CEO support to move forward with strategy discussions for the enterprise.
- An additional ONA project identified the key communicators across the enterprise in response to the employee engagement scores. The CEO acted and identified roundtable participants and Communication Ambassadors to close the communication gaps.
- Additional change initiatives were developed from the ONA results. Leadership from all companies organized the initiatives. There was progress to bridge silos and have cross-functional activities and plans.

Strategy and Leadership

I met with the HR Director of a company that had five different operating companies. He seemed interested in my work and set up a meeting with the CEO. He advised me to develop a proposal in advance that focused on just the leadership of the organization.

The HR Director explained they were holding quarterly leadership development sessions. They were looking for new ideas and methods for leaders to learn about and use to develop their organizations. ONA seemed like a good topic to include in a leadership training/development session at this level.

The CEO was interested in ONA and how it could help his organization. He had enough information from the proposal that outlined the ONA process, value, and outcomes. The CEO was a thoughtful leader, a visionary, and a consensus builder—something I learned once I got to know him better. During the meeting he explained that he was struggling to develop an enterprise strategy that aligned the five companies.

The operating companies were designed to be financially autonomous, and their operations and services were independent of each other. They had their own purpose, goals, and objectives as to how they contributed to the enterprise. The Corporate Services component had oversight and final approval of budgets. Corporate Services included the CEO, HR, IT, Finance, and some PR functions that provided shared services to the operating companies.

The CEO viewed the enterprise as one system that was outward facing to the community and customers. They had one brand with the operating companies supporting it based on their function. The enterprise spanned multiple states on the west coast with some presence in the Midwest.

One operating company was headquartered in a separate state. The rest were headquartered in the same state, where one of the companies was initially founded and started the brand. They were a significant and known part of the local community.

> *The CEO thought there was a valuable enterprise objective to align the companies and their strategies, but some of the company presidents resisted.*

This company started as a family-owned business and had been around for decades. Today it is a 100% employee-owned ESOP. They had significant growth over the years based on the vision started by their founder. They were very successful and grew to be a diversified brand that helped them weather the storm of the economic downfall in 2007 and 2008.

The CEO thought there was a valuable enterprise objective to align the operating companies and their strategies, but some of the company presidents resisted. They each had their own thoughts of how to be aligned but stay autonomous. The CEO was frustrated and had put aside the strategy discussions when we met.

When he understood what ONA could do, he thought it might be a useful method to close the gap and give him leverage to move the enterprise forward. He wanted to ensure they all presented as one company to their customers and to the community. He also wanted to have a competitive advantage while profiting for the employees and supporting the culture for change, growth, engagement, and retention.

He was quiet during the initial meeting while he listened to the overview of ONA. He had a few questions but primarily he listened. After I finished the overview, he made a few notes. The room was silent while we waited to see what he would say.

He looked up and said, "You just explained something to me that I think will help me in different areas of my organization that I am working on. Let's do it!" Of course, I was excited. We moved forward to get everything organized and start the ONA survey.

Working with the CEO to Get Started

The company was just shy of 1,000 employees with 125+ leaders. The CEO wanted to focus on the strategy issue. We developed the ONA survey to include only the leaders. We developed the questions around strategy and purpose for leaders to understand their organization from a different perspective.

The CEO sent out communications to notify the leaders of what we were doing and why. The survey yielded a 100% response rate—what a success! The CEO was happy. People were interested, supportive, and curious about what we were doing and what it would produce.

Once the initial analysis was finished, I met with the CEO to go over the presentation. I had little context to work from and I wanted to be sure I was covering what he wanted and meeting his expectations.

The Main Event

The CEO was involved in preparing the presentation. It was well worth having him involved at this point. In fact, he asked me, "Would it be okay if I chimed in now and then during the presentation?" He was learning and was obviously interested. It made it more fun for me and I respected someone who was interested and grasped what ONA described about his organization.

I told him, "That would be important for the leaders to hear your input. If you want to make a comment or stand up and contribute, just do that at any time. I don't mind at all." He also wanted to talk about the next steps at the end and he developed that information. I welcome any kind of engagement and interaction. It is important to feel comfortable with the data and use it to be confident with the process and the results.

There was one part of the Strategy Network that showed a trusted interaction pattern. I explained the pattern and what it meant for that network. During the presentation, he didn't think I emphasized it enough. He stopped me at that point, got out of his seat, and explained to the leaders, "Look here! See this pattern of communication and interaction? That shows a trusted environment for that company." It made me smile. (See Co. C in Map 5).

What We Learned

Of course, the network we paid the most attention to during the discussion was Strategy. It validated the CEO's intuition and concern about silos across the companies.

The Strategy Network (See Map 5.) looks forward and considers the business direction of the organization. I explained to the group, "As a whole, the organization does not share strategy across the enterprise." Using the map, I explained a couple of situations outlined in the text box insert.

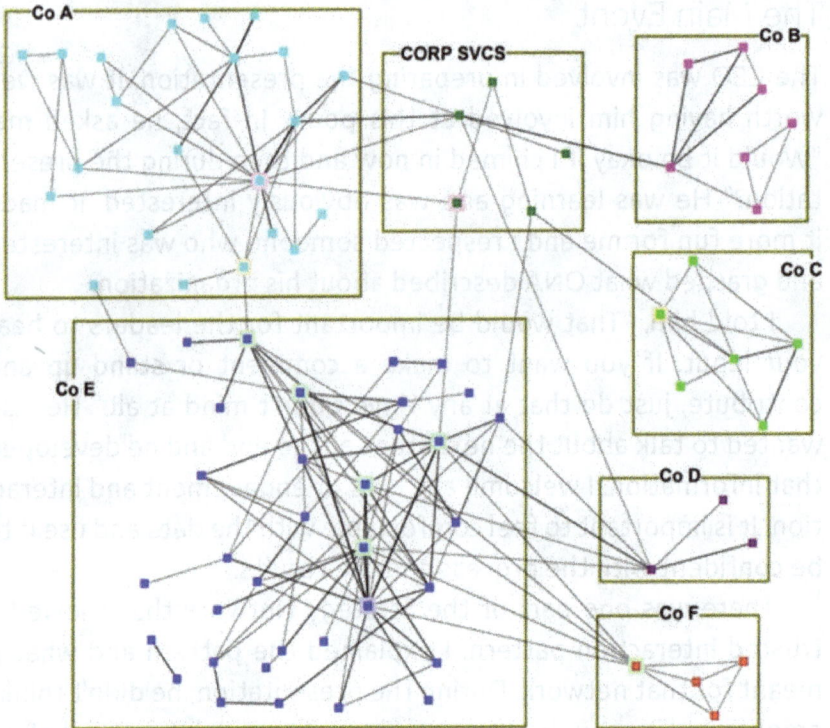

Map 5. Strategy Network

- The Strategy map shows the five operating companies and Corporate Services.
- The question we asked in the ONA survey is shown at the top of the map.
- The colors represent the different companies and Corporate Services.
- Companies D and F report through Company E, so officially there are five.
- The highlighted nodes correspond to the Key Connectors identified for the Strategy Network (see Table 2.)
- The individual operating companies were indeed discussing strategy within the boundaries of their companies, but they weren't sharing it effectively across the enterprise.
- The evidence includes the single connections from Co. B and Co. C to only Corporate Services.
- The other companies had more connections between each other, but still only a few and usually from one person.
- The enterprise was siloed when it came to Strategy.

During the presentation, I encouraged the group to ask questions or challenge me if they didn't agree or had something they wanted to understand further. I said, "Once I leave, there isn't anyone who can explain this, so it is okay to disagree or question me. I encourage questions. I will explain the findings or point out why and where the analysis indicates what is shown in the maps. I will explain what the data is telling me and why I am making the statements that I am."

I went further, "You have the context and details, I don't. That is the rest of the story to understand the data and impact more fully so you can benefit from the analysis and make changes if you choose to. This is the time to share that information so I can hear more from your perspective. I will need the details and context to finalize the maps and make further recommendations."

I didn't know who anyone was in the room other than the CEO, the General Counsel, and the HR Director. One of the Presidents of the five companies was sitting in the back of the room. He stood up and said, "I am upset that you say we don't discuss strategy!" I said, "Ok, tell me why and tell me more about your thinking." He said, "My company does discuss strategy on a regular basis." I asked him, "Which company are you"? He said, "Company C."

I looked at the map, pointed to the pattern of Company C and said, "You are absolutely right! You share strategy within your own company. But look at what is going on. You happen to be the only one from your company that goes outside the boundaries of your company to share the strategy."

I continued, "On top of that, the only person you reach out to discuss strategy with is with the CEO. You don't share your ideas and strategy with members of the other operating companies or the presidents, who are your peers. You are relying on the CEO to have the information and make sense of it and share it with everyone else. That is not how you align an organization.

"So yes, you are doing great! For that matter, so are all the other companies if we only look at what everyone does internally within the boundaries of their company. Each company discusses their strategy in some way within their organization. None of these other companies share it across the enterprise either, at least to the point that it could be called 'shared.' They are going through the C-suite, and in some cases, a few others. It is not being shared openly and transparently."

I continued to explain the impact and consequences that not sharing strategy and misalignment could create. I said, "I don't have any way to prove this, but I think that as a combined enterprise you are losing revenue and opportunities. Eventually, if not already, your brand will be affected, from the customer's perspective. They will perceive or experience a dysfunctional and/or disjointed organization. You want to present your enterprise as a unified brand. You want everyone to know that when they hear your name, they think that it is a great company."

> *The CEO came up behind me and whispered in my ear, "This was awesome." To this day, he still comments that ONA was a good tool for his organization to use.*

"Even though behind the scenes you might all do something different and what you consider unique, the customers don't necessarily know that, nor do they care! They expect the same customer service no matter who they meet with about a project. They come to you because you have a solid reputation, and they expect the same integrity they have experienced from working with one or more of your operating companies."

"If that isn't happening and you are not aligned, you are bound to lose innovation, creativity, strategic and competitive advantage, and customer service/satisfaction. These factors add up to lost revenue." He just looked at me, agreed, and sat down. There were many nods of agreement as I was talking to him.

I will never forget what happened in the end. The CEO came up behind me before I turned it back over to him to close the session. He had the last slide to present for next steps and recommendations that he helped develop. He whispered, "This was awesome." He still comments that ONA was a good tool for his organization to use.

Gaining Context

Later, the CEO asked me to take the key influencers (Table 2) that I identified from the ONA analysis and interview them to provide additional context and feedback. I wrote a report about the findings. The CEO took some of that and worked with the presidents to try and reduce some of the issues they had. Over time, they started a change initiative across the enterprise. There were people from each company that included leaders from the operating companies to form a team and develop key areas to align the enterprise.

Work	Social	Decision	Strategy	Expertise	Innovation	Improvement
A	I	D	G	D	C	C
B	D	N	K	C	O	D
C	N	O	R	G	G	G
D	E	B	A	E	R	I
E	F	C	I	O	D	O
F	N	N	N	N	Q	N
G	O	E	L	I	H	R
H	B	G	F	M	S	E
I	C	Q	D	T	A	M
J	P	H	C	A	K	T
K			S			F
L			E			
M						

Table 2. Key influencers in each network. Color coding is by person to show their presence in multiple networks. For example, node D is a key connector in every network. People change their rank position depending on the metrics from that network calculation.

When I met with the 25 key influencers, many of them commented about how interesting it was to have a visual understanding of their companies and the enterprise as a whole. They also confirmed that it was a true representation of how their organization functions.

The CEO shared the results with the Board of Directors and with the presidents. I met with the Chairman of the Board to explain the purpose and results. I also explained how the information could be used and what the next steps were based on the findings.

A Unique ONA to Find Key Communicators

We also did another form of ONA. The CEO was particularly concerned with employee engagement survey comments about communication. Employees wanted more information and involvement in decisions that affected them.

I created one Network survey question to identify the key communicators across the entire organization. The survey invited 750 employees. Over half of the employees participated. The question was designed to rank order the results based on the responses from the participants. It was also designed not to be a popularity contest.

I gave the CEO a list of the top 80 communicators across all companies and levels. The map is shown below (see Map 6). The companies are color coded.

- The responses primarily grouped together by company with some connections mixing (Company A and F; Company B and E).
- The shapes distinguish management levels (triangles) from non-management levels (circles).
- There is a large aqua circle node that stands out and represents the person that most people selected as the #1 communicator across the enterprise.
- The formula analysis was designed to mitigate it being a popularity result. Also, to mitigate the management level influence.
- Essentially, the larger the circle or triangle the more people nominated them, or nominated others who also nominated them, as someone they had confidence would share information about the organization or knew information they could trust.

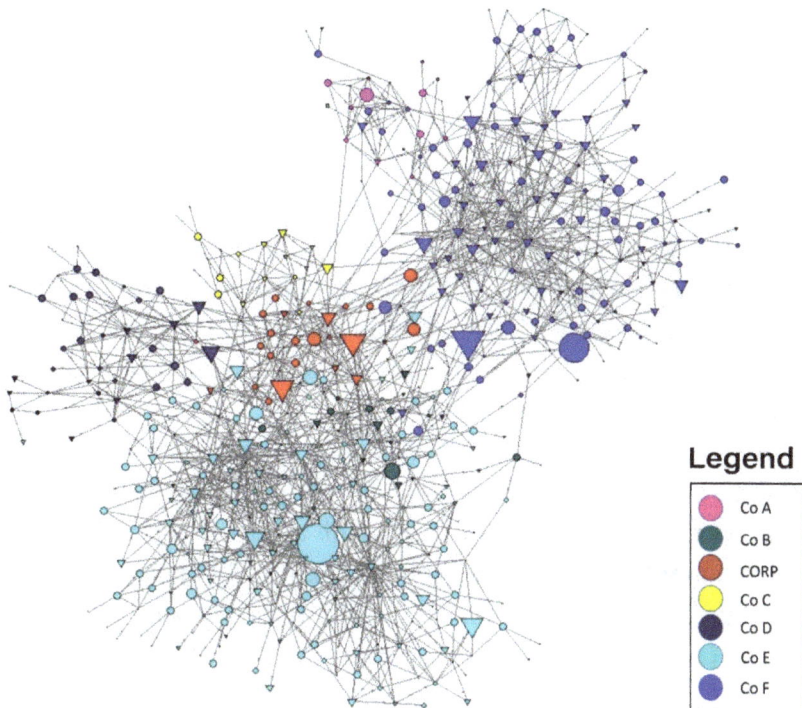

Map 6. Key Communicators by Company

The CEO was intrigued. He expected that most people would select management employees. In many cases they did. The formula took that into account. Once he saw the large aqua circle representing a non-management employee, he asked, "Who is that"? When I identified the person, others in the room shouted, "He is an intern!"

No one expected that, especially the CEO. That is the value of ONA—to uncover some things you might not know about or even suspect about how the work happens, where communication and information flows, and if and where collaboration occurs. Eventually, that intern was offered a full-time job and became even more influential as a key go-to person, perhaps partially since everyone knew who he was now.

The CEO took the list of key communicators and narrowed it to include only employees who were employed for less than three years. He was responding to the employee engagement survey results that indicated communication was an issue across the organization, especially for new employees.

He wanted a solution to close the gap. He was also concerned about turnover, especially with new employees and millennials who were recently hired. He organized several roundtables and met them in person. There were about ten employees from the list in each group. He had an open discussion and invited them to talk about whatever they wanted.

He gave them insight about the company and how much he valued new employees, especially bringing new ideas to the company. The participants reported what a difference it made for them to meet with the CEO who listened to them openly. He followed up to respond to their questions and concerns.

The CEO used ONA effectively to help communication spread across the organization. The action he took impacted the enthusiasm and motivation of the newer employees and others as well. Using the PR team, they shared the experience with all employees.

The CEO knew this focus and effort could increase engagement and retention of employees in general because he'd met with the key communicators and they would share information across the organization. He was getting value and a multiplier effect that he wouldn't have known about without using ONA.

The CEO offered this testimonial, "A very cool process to determine how we communicate as a company. The analysis shows collaborative teams, command and control teams, and people that work effectively throughout the entire company."

4

COLLABORATION AND GENDER BALANCE

OVERVIEW

Problem: An IT leadership team identified employee engagement issues from corporate survey results.

Why: The CIO wanted to get more details about the issues identified in the employee engagement survey and act to resolve them.

What: The IT leadership team requested a custom employee opinion survey coupled with an ONA for a roadmap to make positive change. This was during the pandemic with the entire IT department working from home.

Outcome:

- The employee opinion survey provided over 1,300 comments which provided context to the quantitative results. The comments also helped to correlate the ONA results.
- ONA identified the change agents. An employee Change Agent Team (CHAT©) formed to develop action plans for four major change initiatives identified in the opinion survey. The

goal was to create positive change and improve the survey results.

- Additional ONA results showed the leadership team where there were collaboration and information flow gaps. Lists of key influencers and brokers were developed to build the core network and close the gaps.

- A positive finding was the gender balance within the IT organization that demonstrated diversity inclusion in support of their DEI plans.

Collaboration During the Pandemic

During the pandemic I worked with a healthcare organization. The focus was on the IT department, with about 250 employees. The IT department had gone through a restructuring about four years before. Management identified issues with employee engagement and the culture since the restructuring but there were other contributing factors.

The business was growing fast, and the workload grew to be overwhelming. There was a lot of unrest among the employees. The CIO asked for a custom employee opinion survey and an ONA. The organization had also completed a corporate engagement survey, which didn't produce good results. They wanted to focus on the issues identified in the corporate survey to gain more insight and develop action plans to create positive change.

Two Surveys

The ONA and opinion survey results were used together for context to provide valuable information and perspective. Both surveys were conducted while the entire IT organization was working from home during the pandemic.

Communication had suffered before the pandemic and the issue was magnified during the work-from-home experience. The results from the surveys were eye opening in a couple of areas.

1. This organization defied the odds compared to some empirical research and articles about organizations becoming more siloed during the pandemic. It was unique in that regard. You will see it clearly in the ONA maps later in this chapter.
2. The employee survey comments reported that:
   - Employees really liked the people they worked with.
   - They embraced the mission and values that created the culture of the company.
   - The mission was based on the company's purpose and the customers they served.
   - The employees knew they were helping people and their values matched the corporate values. That was part of the motivation for people to stay, even though the workload was causing some burnout.
   - People were starting to have work-life balance issues that they didn't feel they had before.

Some Surprises

Management and the organization responded quickly to set employees up to work remotely when the pandemic hit. Management didn't like keeping it remote though. They thought virtual work was less productive and expected the employees would report the same through the survey questions.

Management was surprised to learn that 94% of the employees reported that they preferred virtual work options. Employees also responded with 92% favorability that they were more productive working virtually or with flex options.

In fact, when asked, "If you decided to leave the organization, what would be your reasons," many employees responded that if management took virtual work options away, they would look elsewhere. The organization responded accordingly and they offer virtual work options to this day. Management realized this was an important factor for retention and for recruiting, especially in IT.

There were many issues identified in the employee survey that needed attention. I wrote a substantive report that included the results and suggested action plans for each of the surveyed categories. It was important that they not delay and act immediately. That didn't occur, partially due to client demands. It was critical for the necessary changes for management to act and re-engage employees.

ONA Can Help

One of the complaints from the opinion survey was lack of communication across groups. They were functioning with a silo mentality—which could be attributed to the IT leadership—and they weren't aligned. After seeing the ONA results, they are beginning to see themselves as interdependent units. ONA showed a couple main findings.

ONA indicated a hierarchical organization in most of the maps and through the metric analysis. The leaders confirmed that most of the promotions were from within. That is neither bad nor good. However, it can create, and in this case did, technical people who become leaders who don't let go of their "expert" status.

Remember the story in Chapter 2, about using ONA for coaching? The technically proficient employee was promoted to management and wanted to maintain his Subject Matter Expert (SME) status. Experts have a hard time letting go since that likely is why they were promoted. However, experts don't always make good managers, unless they effectively make the transition and shed their SME status.

At any management level, but especially at a director level, leaders need to delegate and empower others. There were comments in the employee survey that this was an issue and negatively impacted the empowerment and authority of the developers and other employees to make decisions. The ONA maps confirmed this.

The leadership showed up as the backbone in the networks (see Map 7a). One example was the Improvement Network. I used it to highlight for the leaders how their organization was functioning because of their organization structure and leaders' attitudes. They had the option to keep it like it was or change it.

When I do the initial analysis and present the results, I am looking for context. There isn't a right or wrong with the results. ONA presents the reality of how their organization functions. If people are unhappy and report issues, the ONA offers objective data and associated analysis. That information can be used to start making changes. ONA shows it clearly. Most of the leaders resisted changes. Most of them were still acting as SMEs.

Q: Who do you consult when you want to overcome obstacles or improve things?

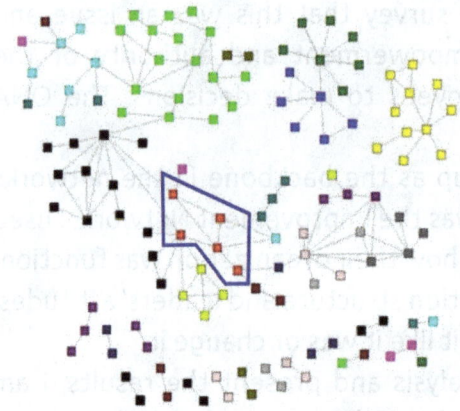

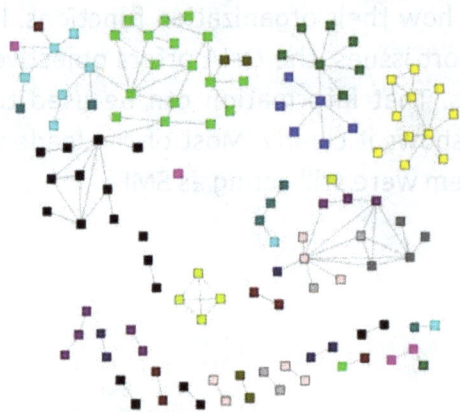

Map 7a. The Improvement Network. The network on the top shows a group of five red nodes in the middle of the core network. They are the five directors of the IT organization.

Most of the other people that the functional leaders connect with are management levels. The Improvement Network for this organization is dominated by management-level employees and a few non-management employees.

The multitude of smaller clusters at the top right and pairs of employees at the bottom who have improvement ideas are disconnected from the core and have no path to share their ideas.

Map 7b. The same Improvement Network on the bottom has those five leaders removed and you see how disconnected the remaining network becomes.

The Improvement Network is a higher trust network. It is important that someone with an idea has a connection they trust with a path to someone who will hear the idea and do something about it. Otherwise, ideas get lost, ignored, or become one-offs.

In a hierarchical organization like this, they have no avenue for their ideas to reach a decision maker unless they have formed a trusted relationship with their direct management.

Other Requested Information

I also gave the leaders a list of key influencers to compare to their succession planning HIPOs lists. They did make a few changes using the ONA list since it produced some surprising insights. In addition, I developed a list of people who could bridge the networks to reach across and bring others in so the organization could develop their core.

It is important to build and strengthen the core to provide organizational resiliency if there is major change or turnover. The organization could fall apart if key influencers left the organization. The key influencers are identified using ONA and provide risk management or recovery ideas.

On a positive note, the employees were collaborating during the pandemic and ONA confirmed this. There were many comments in the opinion survey that most employees liked working with each other. This helped them stay engaged within their teams and project groups. On the other hand, the quantitative results reported employees felt left out of the information flow from leadership, especially related to decisions that affected them.

Gender Balance

From a gender diversity perspective, this was a well-balanced organization (see Map 8). Unfortunately, HR didn't approve collecting other demographics to measure diversity. Employees were sensitive about sharing demographic information, which stemmed from the distrust developed during the previous restructuring.

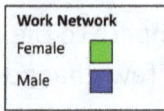

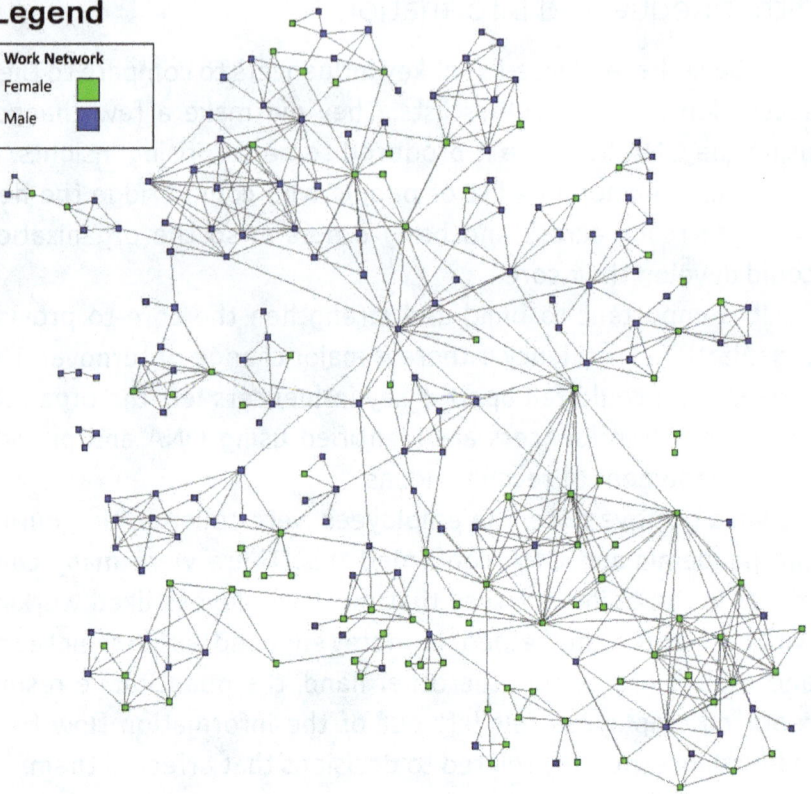

Map 8. Gender Work Network. The Work Network indicates a collaborative IT department that is also equitably balanced and interactive by gender. This was a positive indicator for the IT department. It is a substantive measure for DEI beyond the number of males/females.

Inclusion and Equity is more about being integrated into projects, the culture, and workgroups, not just filling a seat. ONA is the method to really understand DEI in your organization.

Change Agent Value

The opinion survey indicated many issues. It was critical to respond and act to the concerns and comments from the opinion survey. After time passed with no action from leadership, I recommended forming a Change Agent Team.

I had created and implemented the CHAT concept years before by synthesizing organizational change management models and processes. It was very successful and warmly received by leadership and non-leadership employees. This organization implemented it in a slightly different way but still using the change agents identified from the ONA results.

ONA has the advantage of identifying "real" change agents. Most change agents are selected using a subjective method based on who is available or who is assigned by the managers. Often, managers are assigned as the change agents. That is not optimal for a lot of change management reasons.

From an ONA perspective, "real" change agents are those that are integrated, influential, and collaborative across the networks/ organization. Change agents are identified through combined ONA metrics. I organized a non-management CHAT group that could address the key areas of focus for positive change.

Leaders used the employee opinion survey results, including the open-ended comments, to define the focus areas. Part of the process included inviting all employees to validate some of the employee comments and suggestions from the survey. CHAT members developed communication methods to reach out to their respective groups and invite employee participation.

The CHAT developed action plans that were specific, directly applicable to the topic area, and manageable for this organization. Employee involvement in decisions that affect them yields better solutions and suggestions for improvement. The resulting action plans have a better chance of success and sustainability.

In fact, one of the lowest-scoring quantitative prompts from the custom survey reflected just that: the employees rated it low based on their being excluded from decisions that affected them. It said, "*When decisions are made, the people affected are asked for their ideas.*" That prompt's response was 57% favorable.

The explicit plan to invite employees to participate would help with that—assuming the leadership team would support CHAT and embrace their recommendations.

> *CHAT is helping to change the attitude of the employees, slowly. For the action plans to become part of positive change and make an impact, leadership needs to act.*

Action Plans

We scheduled CHAT meetings to work on action plans starting with four major initiatives identified from the employee opinion survey. The action plans were presented to the leadership with recommendations to institute the plans throughout the IT culture and organization.

CHAT helped to change the attitude of the employees, slowly. It hasn't improved substantially yet but there is progress. We also developed sustainability suggestions for CHAT. One suggestion to sustain the work of CHAT was to develop mini projects so all employees could volunteer and contribute to positive change. They were already getting requests from employees to either participate in CHAT directly or support them in some way.

ONA made a difference by involving key employees who had influence with other employees. As a result, leadership paid more attention to what CHAT recommended. For the action plans to become part of positive change and make an impact, leadership needs to act. Employees are hoping for positive change, but they realize the organization structure and leaders can create a roadblock for change.

ONA can only raise awareness of reality. It is up to leadership to use the information effectively for their organizations.

5

CAREER PATH, KNOWLEDGE TRANSFER, AND GENERATIONS

OVERVIEW

Problem: HR and the CEO knew that several baby boomers were retiring soon. They wanted to protect the institutional knowledge that would be leaving the organization.

Why: The CEO wanted a knowledge transfer program. He also wanted to understand what was happening about career advice for the apprentice engineers.

What: The ONA survey was developed with a focus on career, expertise, and generations.

Outcome:

- ONA identified several millennial engineers who were ready to leave the organization because they didn't think they had a career path.
- ONA identified engineers with surprising customer facing responsibilities—an eye-opener that changed their training plans.

- The Expertise map identified the core issue related to knowledge transfer that affected retention. The CEO and HR VP changed their knowledge transfer program design.
- One of the millennial engineers became a more formal leader to close the collaboration gap and share information/training among the millennial generation group.
- There was significant cost avoidance by retaining the apprentice engineers. Leaders wanted them to stay with the organization.
- There were training cost savings and a focus on organizational learning for the millennial engineers as they shared and solved problems together.

Knowledge Transfer and Collaboration

I met with the VP of HR and the CEO of a manufacturing company. This company used chemicals to develop products for many types of other companies, like Boeing and other airlines and industries. They had Engineers who developed and tested these products.

The HR VP shared the business initiative plans. They thought ONA could provide information to add value to the plans. One of the plans was a knowledge transfer program. Several baby boomers planned to retire soon. The executives wanted to be sure there was time to share their knowledge. The intellectual capital of this organization was valuable, and they didn't want to lose it.

The company also knew that finding and hiring good talent was difficult. They had started an apprenticeship program for engineering graduates from a local university—all millennials. The CEO had recently met with these young engineers. They were asking the CEO about career growth and training.

He told me, "I am confused why all these new engineers don't understand they have to gain experience and wait their turn. I am surprised that so many of them are asking the same question and their managers are as confused as I am about it."

Training and career path are common questions for millennials that can create conflict and confusion between generations. The executives thought the knowledge transfer program would satisfy the engineers, but it was going to take time to start and develop.

The impact of these ideas and the time factor involved would have gone unnoticed without ONA. In fact, before ONA, they didn't realize the ideas were not going to work as they initially thought. Based on the ONA results, they quickly realized that the knowledge transfer program needed to be redesigned. They also needed to respond to the young engineers' career requests.

ONA Made a Difference

ONA identified some surprises. The Expertise Network for this organization was one of the primary networks to explain collaboration and information sharing. The results of the Expertise Network (see Map 9) showed that the millennial engineers were disconnected as a group, even from each other.

The millennials were primarily skipping generations and going to boomers to get information. Most of the boomers were their managers. Perhaps the boomers had the information the millennials needed to learn more and faster. Some research suggests that it was common for one generation to skip a generation to get information and assistance with job performance and advancement.

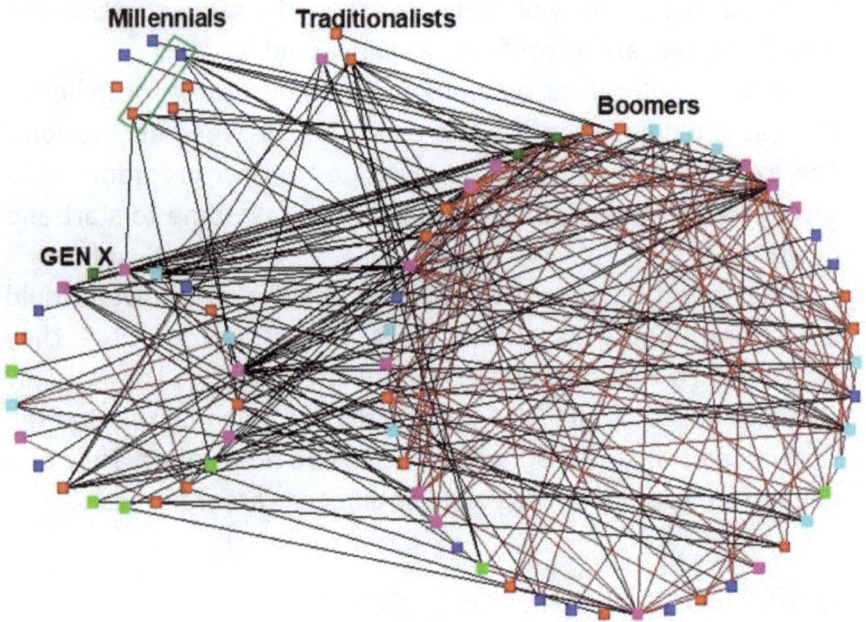

Map 9. The different colored nodes represent the functional departments of the engineering group. The black lines are connections across generations. The red lines are connections within the generations.

In this case, the millennials work in two departments. There is only one pair of millennials, outlined with a green box, that share and communicate about expertise. Most of the expertise connections from millennials is to the boomer group. The traditionalists are still heavily involved in sharing information and expertise across the organization.

The Career Network, the highest trust network, was informative to solve the career request puzzle the CEO faced (see Map 10). The Career Network results displayed individuals who were searching for career advice. They were reaching out to a lot of different people on a regular basis, in this case daily and weekly.

Career discussions are usually long term. This map indicated career plans were urgent for some individuals. The pattern to note, which was the clue for the Career Network, looks like a hub and spoke design, as seen in Map 10. There were three millennials that were prominent in this network. They are the circled nodes.

The connections are directed, meaning one-way connections with arrows. The millennials were reaching out to others to get career advice and information. It is not typical to see a Career Network with this much activity, especially daily or weekly. The thicker the line, the more frequently they connect. Also, the network usually displays pairs or trios that are not connected to others or connected to only a few since career advice is usually sought from special people that someone trusts rather than so many.

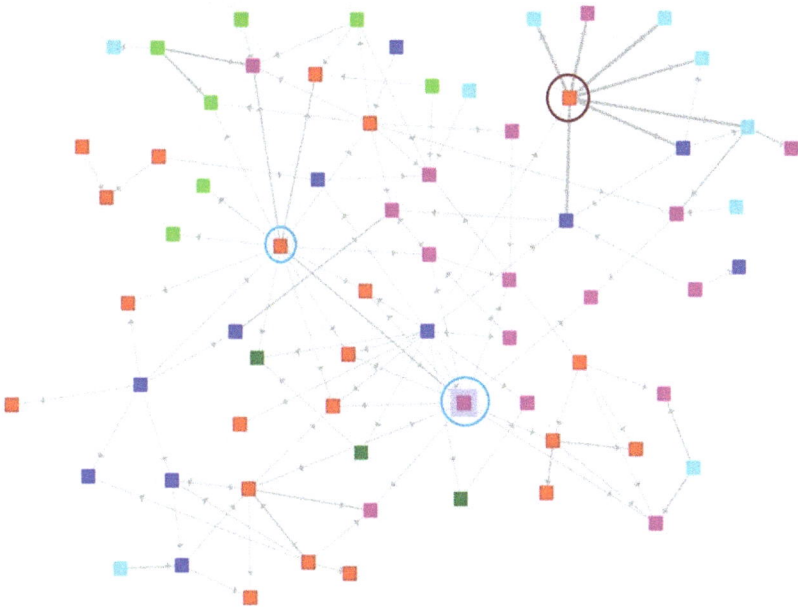

Map 10. Career Network. The arrows show the direction of requests. The nodes circled have almost all lines reaching out to other nodes with few reaching into them. The node circled in red is a millennial engineer who resigned before the results from ONA were available. The thick gray lines indicate a daily request to the individuals he contacted to discuss career options.

The ONA results in this network indicate an employee who is urgently considering career options and who, if not satisfied with the available information, might plan to resign. The two nodes circled in aqua are two other millennial engineers who are reaching out to find out career information. They are not reaching out as frequently, since the links are lighter in color, but it is still a concern for HR and the CEO. Especially since the engineer circled in red already left the organization. The other two might be considering the same.

It was even more telling that one of the millennials was going to several different people. When I pointed out that person, I didn't know he was a millennial. I was commenting about how unusual it was to have someone reaching out so frequently. The HR VP said, "Who is that?" When I told her, she gasped and said, "That person is one of the millennial engineers who left two weeks ago because he didn't think he had a career with us. He felt that his talents should be recognized and rewarded in some way."

The HR VP seemed very concerned about learning this information and she realized they missed the warning signs. ONA uncovered behavior that was critical to address possible issues before they escalated. She immediately asked me for the names of the other engineers that are circled in aqua in Map 10.

She told me, "One is also a millennial engineer, and he is asking for a department transfer. When we finish, I am going to his manager to inform him about what we found. He doesn't want to lose this person from his group, and he is blocking the transfer. I will tell him that we will lose him from the company if we don't let him transfer and to do it immediately!"

Knowledge Transfer Enhanced

I asked the HR VP about the knowledge transfer program plans. She said they were going to have training once they designed the program and involved the retirees. She wanted to know how to use the ONA data so it would be effective and useful for everyone.

She planned to identify who was retiring, what their skill sets were, and to try to figure out how to get their knowledge explicitly stated and shared. I explained, "Since you know the people retiring, you can look at the maps to see who they are connected to. You can match the connections to the expertise of the person retiring and close the gap with training and knowledge sharing. You can also look at the others they have connections with that will be affected or left out when they leave so they can be invited into the conversation and identify what they might need. Document it in some way or interview them to identify important information they should share."

> *They changed the knowledge transfer program and kept the millennials from leaving their organization.*

I added, "More importantly, you need to work with the millennials to connect them to one another for a lot of reasons. They and the organization are losing a lot of the training opportunities and valuable learning they could gain from their peers. They are getting on-the-job training, formal training, or learning about your products and services but they aren't sharing it with each other.

"That is a waste of time and money for your organization. They also lose out on the collaboration, innovation, relationship opportunities, and community they can gain from sharing as a group." She asked me what I would suggest.

"Work with the individual that we identified on the career map. You mentioned you are concerned about him leaving next. Ask him to start setting up some type of social engagement or lunch-and-learn with the other millennials. He can be creative. Let him explore options. You can explain that he is a key influencer and has an important network role for the organization. Ask him to organize and connect the millennials with each other and to other employees. Let him know the purpose is to share information, collaborate, and start to get to know each other."

I recommended this as the priority to respond to their impatience and to buy time until the formal program was available. "That will save you a lot of time and effort. They will get to know each other, develop trust, and share information while learning from each other. It will also increase new ideas and problem solving when they can openly think through situations and not feel isolated or reluctant to ask questions."

They did exactly that. Over time, they changed the knowledge transfer program and retained the millennials. The selected millennial engineer became one of the most engaged and important members of their organization as he gained experience. I also suggested having some of the other key influencers contribute to the design and details of the knowledge transfer program.

They ended up avoiding significant costs by retaining the remaining millennials. They saved recruiting and training costs, at a minimum. They likely increased employee satisfaction and engagement, which was reflected in customer satisfaction and improved customer service.

Also, when I identified how many of the engineers were meeting with customers, the CEO immediately reacted and changed some of those situations. In some cases, he added training in customer service skills. ONA not only met their expectations, but it also exceeded them and saved them a lot of time, money, resources, and pain.

6
ORGANIZATIONAL CHANGE

OVERVIEW

Problem: A new CEO brought in a new leadership team. There was change, resistance, and also questions. There had also been an acquisition four years before with unknown consolidation issues.

Why: The CEO wanted a united organization, and the remaining leaders told him they had integrated effectively. He wanted to understand more. Major change was affecting the organization and he needed alignment.

What: The ONA survey was developed to train leaders about organizational change management. Change agents were identified along with a change readiness survey. The results were shared and used for interactive sessions during the conference.

Outcome:

- ONA identified the change agents for the major change initiative plans.
- ONA identified consolidation concerns. The leaders thought the concerns were resolved.

- The change readiness survey indicated areas where the leaders had differences. The leaders were now more aware and prepared for the changes.
- A custom employee opinion survey confirmed specific issues to address with change.
- Change management was initialized for a major project to develop a more efficient customer support process. This saved them time and money during implementation.

Organizational Change

I worked with a consulting team to develop a business strategy for a healthcare company that serviced Medicare and private insurance for medical equipment, supplies, and infusion. The core company had acquired an infusion company in another state four years before. They had hired a new CEO who was hiring and firing top leaders and reorganizing the company.

I advised them about organizational change management (OCM) and leadership development. They had offsite leadership conferences for networking and development. The CEO asked me to focus on communication and organizational change management as a speaker at the conference.

I developed the presentation to connect current information and the changes they were experiencing directly to their organization and leadership perspectives. The leaders completed a change readiness survey and a five-question ONA survey. I developed a presentation about OCM using their results. They learned what was important to become change leaders. The ONA results identified change agents to help them implement changes more effectively.

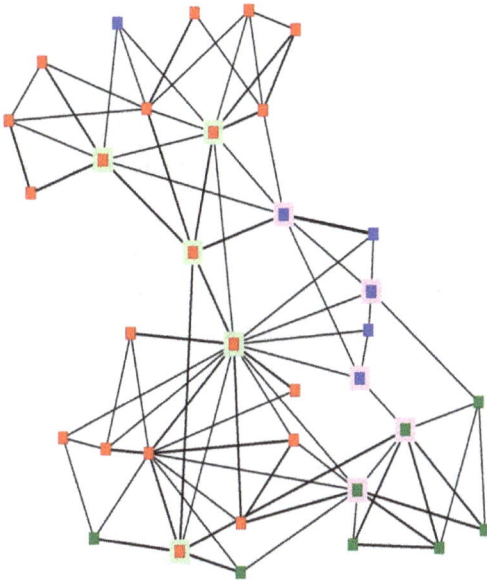

Map 11. The three node colors represent the lines of business for each leader.

The highlighted nodes indicate the change agents. There is good change agent represen-tation from all lines of business that will make the planned changes smoother.

Leadership Pays Attention

I also collected the ONA demographics necessary to display the acquired company separate from the original core business. Map 12 shows the people who were actively reaching across the orga-nization from either of the two companies.

The timing was perfect for the new CEO to gain perspective about the acquisition. The information was valuable to realize how people were working together, or not, in the organization. I was invited to the senior executive staff meeting to present and discuss the ONA information in more detail.

In the meeting, the CEO looked around the room and said, "I asked all of you if the two companies are integrated by now. Deb has some additional information to share with us." Of course, all the leaders were nodding their heads and saying that the compa-nies were fully integrated by now. Yet really, how did they know for sure? I had data to show them that was partially true.

I showed them Map 12 and some others. Once the CEO saw these maps, he seemed surprised and turned to the executives in the room and said, "I thought you told me these companies were working together effectively and were fully integrated. This doesn't look like it to me, not to the extent you indicated and what I thought."

Map 12 shows five out of the eighteen leaders in the acquired organization working with the original core company. The CEO was concerned and said, "We have some work to do!"

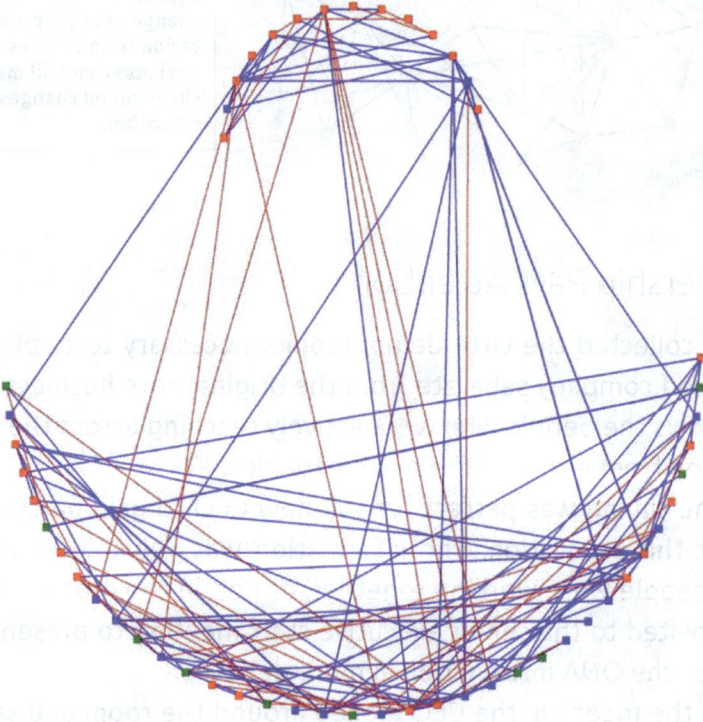

Map 12. The group of nodes at the top represent the leaders in the acquired company. There are only 5 leaders that interact with the leaders in the original core company, shown on the bottom. There are only 14 leaders in the original core company that interact with the acquired company. This was after they were acquired four years before.

The node colors represent the lines of business.

At the conference, they were giving awards and recognition. There was an individual that was retiring who had been there for 25+ years. She was a well-respected leader in the organization. I wrote down her name and offered to develop a map of what it would look like when she left the organization.

They could use the ONA results to determine who she was directly connected to and who would be most affected when she resigned. The information would guide her successor to know who had information they might need. They could close the gap and lower the impact of any institutional knowledge loss when this person left.

Her immediate boss said, "Please go ahead and put together the information for this person and help us understand who she worked with so we can do focused knowledge transfer before she leaves." I explained that is one way to use the ONA results when you know someone is leaving or has resigned.

ONA can identify who will be affected when an individual leaves. ONA can help support those who remain in the organization and who might be wondering, "Well now who am I supposed to turn to for the information and knowledge?" There are often isolated people that no one realizes relied on the individual who left. The isolated people can lose productivity and effectiveness or decide to leave as well if they are not supported or don't feel included.

Unintended Consequences

There is a type of challenge that leaders often don't recognize or pay attention to whenever there is a downsizing, an RIF, or when employees leave the organization. The employees who are left behind evaluate how the organization and how the leaders handle those circumstances. This happens even more so when there is a restructuring, a change initiative, or some type of downsizing. Remaining employees might ask:

- Do they care about the employees leaving and show respect?
- Do they treat the employees who are still there with respect and provide support?
- Do they give the employees information and tools to move forward?
- Do they keep the communication lines open and transparent so those affected aren't left wondering who or if anyone will answer their questions?

Depending on the circumstances, there can be a grieving process because the remaining employees have lost someone they care about, they value, and someone who impacted what they did. If no one provides direction and guidance about how to carry forward, that affects their view of the organization and the leaders as well as their job performance.

Often the employees are left to figure it out on their own. Some leaders assume there is no impact, or they might not know what to do themselves. They likely haven't been trained to know the importance of supporting the remaining employees. ONA is a valuable resource under these types of circumstances. ONA clarifies that it is not solely the direct work relationships that are affected.

Leaders often don't realize what other downstream impact their decisions might create. For example, if there is a change in the work group, or when an employee leaves the organization, it is important to notify the members of the affected work group. It is also important to notify other work group members that are impacted. ONA can tell you who is directly affected and who is affected downstream or indirectly.

The healthcare organization used the ONA results, as well as the change information, to train the leaders and improve their communication. They also gained important information to improve the consolidation of the two companies and protect institutional knowledge when someone leaves.

7

CULTURE AND VALUES

OVERVIEW

Problem: 64% of an organization's workforce was about to retire in a five-year period.

Why: The executive leader wanted to sustain the values and culture of the organization while considering the impact to other factors such as hiring, training, retention, promotions, and development.

What: The ONA survey was designed to project the impact to the organization over a ten-year timeframe. That data was correlated with the technical skills and job roles by person and function. Change agents were identified to help with information sharing. Interviews with some of the change agents provided insight into how people were responding to change and expectations.

Outcome:

- ONA identified the key influencers and change agents that are important to hold the culture together during a major change and transition.

- Developed projections for a ten-year period to understand unintended consequences for those leaving and how it might affect the remaining employees in the organization.
- The leader used the ONA information to assist with project training needs, make promotion process changes, review hiring practices, and streamline them to accommodate a more aggressive hiring process.
- ONA information helped to understand the impact of the institutional knowledge loss and to preserve the culture to carry the mission forward.

Transformation in an Organization While Maintaining Values

I have been fortunate in my work to be introduced to first responder organizations. The leader of this particular first responder organization knew it was facing a massive retirement over a five-to-six year period. He was concerned knowing that he would lose 64% of the organization in that timeframe. It would affect them financially, but that wasn't the major concern.

There were limitations to what he could control regarding the dates of retirement. He knew the skilled resource loss would severely change the organization if he didn't try and mitigate the risk. He wanted to do what he could to sustain their objectives, values, and culture while serving the community to the standards they lived by.

Their values were their culture and the leader had worked hard and diligently to create a sustainable and engaged workforce. He had the option to retire, but he chose not to leave during this critical time. He wanted to lead them through the workforce crisis. It was important to him.

This first responder organization reported to the city and participated in the state retirement system. About 15 years before, the city acquired this private first responder company and brought it into the municipality. This created the retirement dilemma. All the employees started at the same time, which set them up to have the same retirement dates in the state system.

The leader initially addressed the challenge from a budget perspective since he knew that he would have to hire and train many people. He also knew that some processes and methods would need to change, and he wasn't sure how to go about it. He knew he had to look at this problem in a different way.

How We Started

I met with the leader and the two individuals who were his direct reports. They explained how their organization was structured, what happened on a day-by-day basis, their objectives, mission, vision, and goals and how they interacted with the community.

I learned about the unique style of the leader that I would work with and realized that was key to understanding the organization. They explained the urgency of the situation. They emphasized the importance of maintaining their culture and values.

Culture for this organization was how people interacted, collaborated, responded to calls, followed procedures, and shared information. It was about their norms and values. The leader wanted to protect that as much as possible as employees retired, and new ones were hired.

We launched the ONA survey with about 276 employees included. We had a 94% response rate. They provided additional valuable information for comparison and to combine with the ONA results. Such things as their certifications and training per rank and individual.

This enhanced the analysis and usefulness of the ONA results. It was clear how important it would be to fill those positions quickly and get people trained and experienced faster. Not to mention the intellectual capital that would be leaving the organization.

A Bit Different ONA Approach

My approach mapped and analyzed how the organization culture looked today and compared that to how it would look in ten years. I created a map by year of who was expected to retire. Then I took the identified retirees out of the organization map progressively through year ten.

Maps 13 and 14 show the before and after culture view. The after view demonstrated what the culture looked like with 64% of the workforce removed. They would hire people in the meantime, but it was important for them to have the visual impact of what it might look like and the worst-case scenario if they did nothing. That was important for the city manager to understand.

The retirees were highly skilled and many were in key positions. ONA provided an impactful visual of the institutional knowledge leaving the organization. I combined it with more detail, by year, of the associated expertise that included training, certifications, titles, years at levels, and qualifications of individuals retiring by year to show the holes that would be created year by year.

This is an example of combining the human capital information with the social capital from ONA. This depth of information, as it related to the ONA results, gave them a heads up on how to prepare for recruiting, hiring, training, onboarding changes, and promotional opportunities. These were leverage points to preserve their values and stabilize the workforce commitment and engagement as they experienced a lot of change and uncertainty.

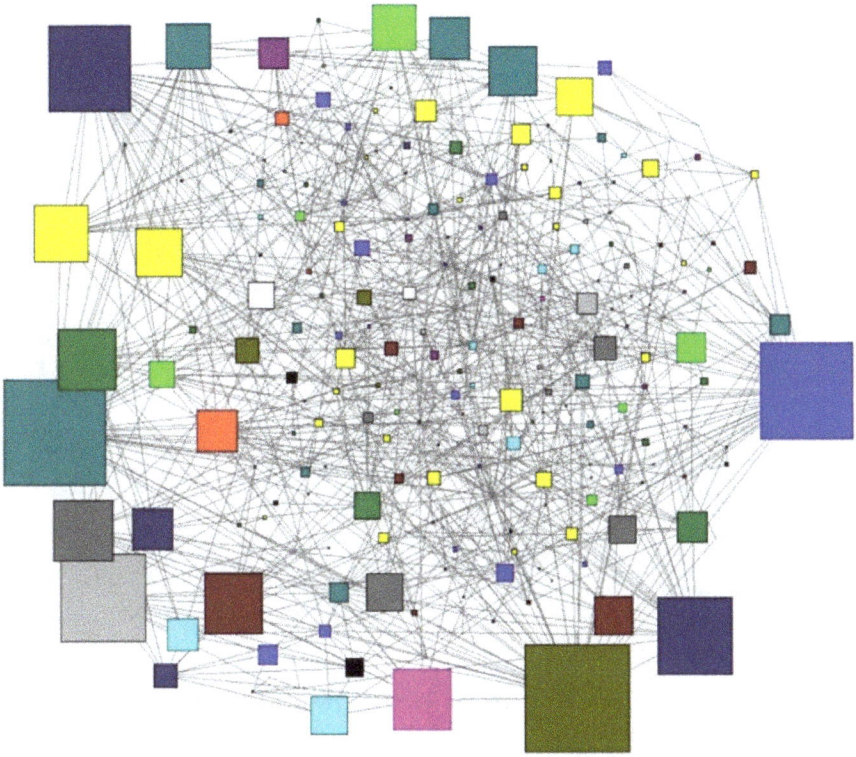

Map 13. The initial organization view of the Work Network. The nodes are color coded by retirement year. The size of the squares indicate how integrated that individual is in the Work Network. You can see from the drastic change in Map 14, they are losing some significant intellectual capital when these individuals retire.

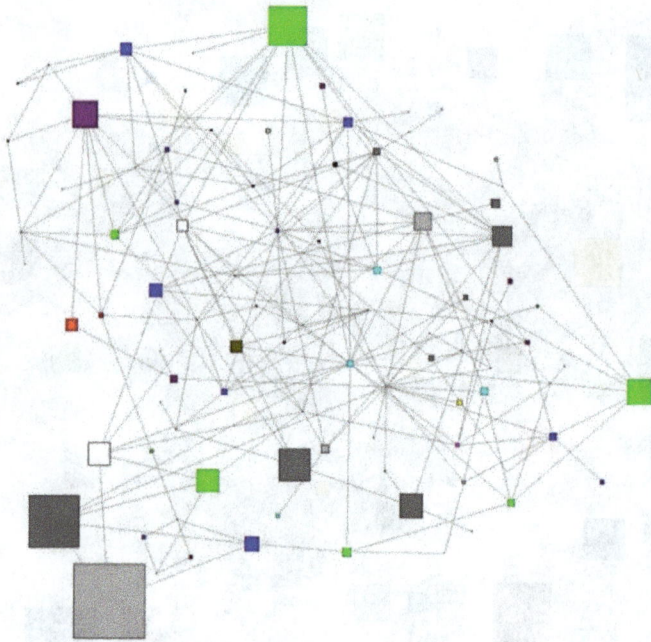

Map 14. The Work Network with 64% of the workforce removed due to retirement.

An Amazing Reaction

Once I completed the analysis, I presented the results to the three leaders. I showed them the Work Network first (see Map 15). The node shapes reflect generations. The node size is based on the integration metric's results. Integration means who has the best access and visibility to information flow and connections in the network.

ONA uses this metric to demonstrate who really knows what is going on in that network and can be influential. The Work Network is the foundation of organizational knowledge and is primarily a transactional network that tells us how the organization functions today. The Work Network is important to this organization.

When I present the initial results to clients, they usually respond with keen and focused interest and excitement. These three leaders were no different. They were very enthused to understand visually how their organization functions. They were out of their seats with the first map and talking about what it meant.

I think that is the value of ONA. It is visual and makes sense once I explain what the colors and shapes mean. They absorb the information and realize how important it is to understand their organization in this way. It fills in a lot of gaps for leaders to make informed decisions and create positive change.

The leaders started pointing to the colored shapes, the nodes that represent individuals in the organization, looking at the names and connections. The "a-ha"s started coming from them. It was amazing to have this much enthusiasm and understanding right from the start without much explanation from me at first.

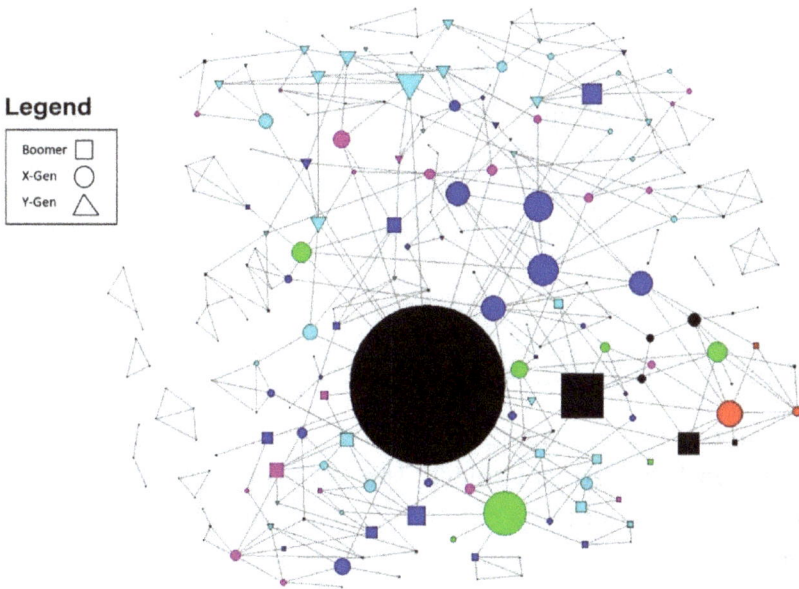

Map 15. Work Network. The colors represent level/titles. The shapes are generations. The different sizes for the shapes indicate who is most integrated in the Work Network.

I was listening to their interaction and taking notes that helped me fill in the context. I heard them saying things like, "I didn't realize I would see this group interacting like that," or, "I didn't know this individual was so important to their group."

There is a natural inclination to find yourself on the maps and how you compare to others. People often think they are supposed to be more connected than they might be.
I explain that it isn't a popularity contest and is different from social media where more connections are considered better. ONA data is rich, deep, insightful, and valid since it comes directly from all the employees. It is a baseline of the reality of the organization at the time. People naturally have a visceral reaction.

Sometimes people think they would have shown up as more key than they ended up being. That isn't the point but a common reaction. Since organizations are dynamic, it will change over time. With ONA, you have an opportunity to guide it in the direction you would like. If you don't purposefully guide it, changes will occur naturally based on how people interact and the relationships they develop.

What the Information Identified

As you can see in Map 15, the nodes are different sizes. That is based on the metrics I select. The large black circle was a surprise to the leader as he didn't realize this individual was that key overall. The other leaders, his direct reports, helped him look at it from others' perspectives rather than his as the leader of the organization and how he experienced this person.

They said, "He likely interacts differently with you as the leader than with his peers and those who report to him. He is engaged, respected, and someone that others go to. That is important information for you, as the leader, to know and understand." He accepted that.

Then the leader decided to focus on his own connections and influence and was concerned that he, as the leader, should show up more integrated in the organization. His node was among the smaller nodes. That is a common and natural reaction, so I was sensitive to his concern. However, I didn't have to say a word.

The others explained, "Are you kidding me? This validates your leadership style that you have worked hard to demonstrate trust, servant leadership, and to reduce your prominence and influence just because you are the leader." They continued to explain, "You are purposely driving decisions deeper into the organization and developing others to become leaders, and this validates your approach and supports your efforts. It is working."

This leader is known to say to the entire organization, "Until you get to know me as a leader, don't trust me, watch me." That is a brave statement. He has proven his integrity and he "walks the talk." Because he has developed such a great culture and lives the values, he can comfortably focus his energy externally to represent his organization to the community and to the city leader in a positive manner. I am honored to have met a leader with integrity, purpose, and such caring for his organization.

His direct reports confirmed to him, "That is why you are a good leader because you don't have to be the center of attention and the hub of the network or the individual that everyone must go to before we get anything done. Your value is as the face of our organization externally, representing the community, the PR side, which you do very well. Therefore, you are not 'needed' in the organization as others are carrying the load for you. This validates that you are successful in that regard."

He changed his perspective about how he was interpreting the initial results and now he laughs about how he reacted. He gave me permission to share that reaction to use as an example for others to relax from a similar reaction. I have earned the title of "Dot Lady," which I accept proudly. For me, that means ONA made an impact and when I am introduced as such, they know what it means.

Invite the Skeptics In

Before the ONA survey could be distributed to the employees there was a key leader that was important to the process. I share this part of the story to help you realize there is often skepticism or resistance to any consulting project, but especially something new or unknown like ONA.

> *I knew this individual could stop the process. It was important for him to be on board and supportive. If he didn't agree to do this, then others would likely resist.*

Initially this individual was resistant. He was protective of the culture, the relationships, and the employees. He felt loyalty and pride and was concerned about someone from the outside coming in to ask what he considered probing questions. He didn't like some of the ONA survey questions.

I knew this individual could stop the process. It was important for him to be on board and supportive. One of the leaders I was working with to launch the project called and let me know this individual wasn't sure about the questions I was asking. He said, "Could you get on the phone and discuss the questions with him?" I said, "No, I think I need to meet with him face to face."

I had never met this person and didn't know what to expect. I sensed he would be a tough sell. I knew others probably trusted him based on his tenure and position. If he didn't agree to do this, then others would likely resist. My intuition about him turned out to be true.

A Critical Meeting for Success

When this key leader walked in the room, he was skeptical of me and the reason I was there. I knew we had to get past this somehow. He explained that the organization was family oriented and they took care of each other. It was personal to him. He made it clear to me that I was an outsider and not one of them. He questioned what I was doing. I respected this perspective and knew I had to earn his trust and commitment.

I asked him what he thought we were going to do, hoping to get him talking and comfortable. I wanted him to know his perspective mattered and I wanted to hear what it was. He said, "I have seen this type of thing before, and it is basically a personality test." I responded, "It really isn't about that, but let me show you more about it. I think it is very important that you support and understand what we plan to do." I shared several maps as examples and explained what ONA could do for them. I made some progress and he started to relax.

I said frankly, "Listen, I will never be one of you. That just isn't possible. So how do we get around that and what can I do to earn your trust?" He said, "I don't understand some of the questions, but one in particular I don't like and I don't understand why you have to ask that question." I gave him a copy of the questions and went through them. I explained what I would do with the information and how it helped me with the analysis.

Then I focused on the question he mentioned that bothered him and said, "If you don't like that question, let's take it out." He looked at me and said, "You would really do that? You would take this question out?" I responded, "Yes, I will. I would like to have it to correlate with other data, but the other questions are more important. If you are willing to leave the rest in, let's take this one out."

I knew that listening to his concerns, understanding them, and demonstrating my integrity was critical for his acceptance. I think that was the turning point. It made the difference to listen and try to understand and accommodate his concern.

I asked about the other questions. "Is there anything we need to edit that improves them for you?" He said, "Yes, I don't know why they need to be so wordy." I said, "Okay, let's go through each one and make some changes." We made edits on the spot, so the questions were simple and to the point.

He was happy and agreed that he would participate in a video with the executive leader and explain to the rest of the employees what I was doing. He would encourage them to participate. He left with a positive attitude and the sample maps to use in the video.

The leader and this key individual made the video. We included it in the email invite for the ONA survey for people to watch and understand why they should participate. The ONA survey got a 94% participation response. I credit him for most of this response and appreciate his cooperation.

> *"This data will be helpful with what we are doing and going through.*
> *It is so different from any other data we have. It is going to fill in gaps for us and be useful for us long term. I love it!"*

Pleasant Surprise

There might have been another skeptic. The other leader of the three I initially met wasn't involved during the project start and set-up process. When I presented the results, he was the first one out of his seat. When I was finished, he turned around and surprised me with his enthusiasm and response.

He said, "This is the best thing I have seen. This data will be helpful with what we are doing and going through. It is so different from any other data we have. It is going to fill in gaps for us and be useful for us long term. I love it!" I hadn't been sure how the leaders would react since they had a unique problem to solve.

They used the ONA results to expand their thinking about the organization and what they faced. They used it to assist with changes in training, recruiting, hiring, and promotional processes. They also recognized the importance of involving the organization.

They included the change agents and brought them into the process. I conducted interviews with some of the change agents to get their impressions of what they were facing and how willing the organization seemed to be about change. The added information was also eye opening and useful.

ONA assisted in raising awareness to understand they could mitigate the risk of their situation. They were more confident moving forward. This project finished right before the pandemic took hold. They had to focus on work demands. Now we are taking the plans further.

We are starting another ONA to dig deeper into supporting their upcoming leaders and developing them quickly. They will be supporting the organization as retirees take their leave. Retirement is happening now and will increase for some time. We will use the ONA social capital understanding to compare to the human capital behavioral assessment information they are also using to assist with development.

The leader of this organization realizes the burden of the changes in the workforce as they relate to cost, resources, and many other factors. ONA is a significant step to mitigate the risk and help to moderate some of the costs.

8

MERGERS AND ACQUISITIONS

OVERVIEW

Problem: Two examples: Leaders in two different organizations each acquired another company to integrate into their organization. They didn't have data to know if it was effective or not.

Why: The leaders wanted to understand how effective the consolidations were after years had passed.

What: In both cases, the ONA survey was developed for other purposes but could also evaluate and display the consolidation and cultural integration progress.

Outcome:

- In the first example, the ONA results indicated that the breadth and depth of the consolidation did not validate what leaders reported to the new CEO.
- In the second example, the ONA results indicated that the breadth and depth of the consolidation was better than the leaders expected and what they thought was occurring.

- In the second example, ONA did verify that the employees in the original core organization were not as proactive as newly acquired organization employees were to integrate the two organizations. The leaders admitted their ideas and communication about the acquired organization had to change.

Human Capital Risk Management

ONA can be categorized as human capital risk management. It evaluates individuals differently than most human capital analysis methods. ONA is one of the most valuable tools you can use to understand your organization as an ecosystem but also to connect it to your bottom line and business objectives. Risk management affects your bottom line and business objectives.

Mergers and Acquisitions (M&A) continue to be a large part of many industries, yet a large percentage still fail for many reasons. I've done research over the years to apply ONA for M&A initiatives. It is clear to me that the main reason for failure is because of issues essential to the consolidation process, especially as they relate to the impact on the employees involved.

Combining separate company cultures is not an easy task. It is usually left until after the merger is legally complete. Considering it is important to merge and integrate cultures for the merger to be successful, here are some of the questions that are answered with an ONA Merger and Acquisition (M&A) project:

> ➤ *How can we reduce the potential for failure of this M&A project?*
> ➤ *How can we reduce the integration issues and costs?*
> ➤ *How can we understand and measure the impact if we need to reduce the workforce?*
> ➤ *How can we understand the impact of restructuring the organizations when we combine them?*

> ➤ *How can we integrate different cultures? Which culture will dominate and why?*
> ➤ *Who can we include as change agents to mitigate resistance and integration issues?*
> ➤ *Who should we know about in the organization who is influential that we might not be aware of?*
> ➤ *What groups/departments/project teams will be most affected and how?*
> ➤ *How can ONA help us set priorities and retain employees?*

Human Capital is Neglected

I gave a presentation several years ago to an eclectic business audience. There were several financial professionals there and many decision makers from different industries. I was invited to present my work about ONA in relation to mergers and acquisitions.

Most people responsible for due diligence in M&A deals only focus on the legal and financial issues. Yet, the organizations to be acquired or to merge with another company all have employees and a culture that comes with the deal. The investors or current management usually determine how best to restructure the organization and management team once the deal is announced or shortly thereafter.

It is common for over 50% and up to 80% of M&A initiatives to fail. They usually fail because of the people issues that inevitably show up sooner or later. The deal-makers usually don't know what to do about the people.

The decisions about structure and organization role and responsibility are usually based on organization charts, employee titles/roles, and subjective opinions from management. They often don't consider the value employees offer or contribute to the organization.

Why? Because most of the time, they don't know about that information or how to get that information beyond their limited view and understanding of the employee roles and contributions. Often, they barely know employee names and roles beyond the organization chart.

They look at the functions represented in each organization and begin to move boxes around thinking this will suffice. To this day, it is common for over 50% and up to 80% of M&A initiatives to fail. They usually fail because of the people issues that inevitably show up sooner or later. I posed the problem to the audience.

"If you are spending all this time, money, and effort to do the legal and financial due diligence, then why don't you include what I call workforce due diligence? You are leaving out important data to make thoughtful and objective decisions that affect the newly formed organization. Often, it is the people issues and culture integration that really cause the deal to fail, and you will likely not achieve your financial objectives if they are not addressed in a timely manner."

Most of the answers were that they didn't know what to do and so they left the human capital part for later and thought it would work itself out. Usually, it didn't, or it took an extended amount of time. As a result, they faced revenue losses, customer dissatisfaction, employee engagement dips, productivity decline, unforced retention issues, and investment losses.

I made a case for how ONA could mitigate the human capital risks of M&A decisions. Granted, sometimes the due diligence might have to wait for the deal to close if there is a *quiet period* or time when no one can discuss the deal. Certainly, taking surveys or collecting employee data to the degree needed for ONA in advance of the deal could break the confidentiality agreements.

It could also cause undue distress to the organization since people might suspect they will lose their jobs, even if that isn't true. People might expect that anyway. At a minimum, there is productivity dips and unrest when people learn about major changes. It could affect their careers and livelihood.

There is still an opportunity to mitigate the risk after the deal closes and before the consolidation issues become severe or too complex. Since M&A deals are about risk assessment, you can insert the ONA process to find options to mitigate the risk. The solution is ONA as human capital risk management and a supplement to the workforce due diligence.

Workforce Due Diligence Ignored

Sometimes HR is involved, or the negotiating companies hire consultants to do some type of due diligence regarding the people and positions involved. Either way, it often involves only high-level decisions and relies primarily on the management people involved in both companies. In most cases, they rely on management-level perception and opinions of who should remain in the organization or how the structure should look.

Often, the decision makers only focus or care about the management/executive levels in the discussion and leave the rest of the organization to either work itself out or for after the deal closes. This sets up integration issues, which often include process and procedure changes and other details. This creates chaos and ambiguity that can be unmanageable for longer than desired.

A Hewitt Associates study suggests that less than 10% of management time is devoted to the human side during due diligence of an M&A. Why is that? They often assume there is cultural compatibility rather than assessing or testing it. Maybe they don't know what to ask or how to really determine if there is cultural compatibility.

There are many examples of M&A failures, yet it doesn't stop people from repeating the same mistakes. Decision makers also believe there is nothing that can be done about it so they just let it play out. They leave it to HR or those in management to figure it out.

Many deals fail from a revenue/investment perspective because the integration fails. It can fail because people resist. People resist because they weren't considered in the preliminary analysis of whether the deal will work or not. It creates fear, uncertainty, and doubt that shows up in lower productivity, engagement, and retention.

The people networks that ONA analyzes and makes tangible influence the success or failure of any change, but especially major change initiatives. It only takes 5% of the key influencers to sway it either way. Use ONA to manage the risk and create a better chance of success. Find out who the key influencers and change agents really are. Don't rely on your intuition for something this important.

> *Eventually the poor decisions show up when the two organizations try to combine their cultures and can create confusion and chaos.*

The issues will show up when the two organizations try to combine different cultures. Decision makers rely on a narrow understanding of how the organization functions. They move forward without objective data to know how people work together or the impact that such a dramatic change has on the organization and the culture.

Let's Go Forward With ONA

Workforce due diligence using ONA is a good idea for M&A. It is especially important for private investors since they usually want to protect and recover their investment as quickly as possible.

They often install a management team or consultants to guide the direction of the business.

Take the time to conduct an ONA after the deal closes and before the consolidation gets too far along. It provides the new management, investors, and/or consultants with a roadmap of rich information. It saves a lot of headaches, frustration, time, and money.

You gain so much knowledge about all the employees and how to efficiently move forward more quickly. You gain a baseline for measuring change and uncover gaps or challenges you could face. It is a workforce road map that has valuable information to set priorities, plans, and strategies.

Workforce due diligence does not directly assess if the transaction will or should take place. The process provides information on how to make it more successful and mitigate risk. The workforce due diligence information can be added to the legal and financial due diligence to consider for the final decision.

At a minimum, it can help create a checklist for focus when you are ready to do the ONA. Some of the workforce risks to consider include:

- Underestimating the difficulties of merging two cultures
- Departure of key people—voluntary or involuntary
- Expenditure of too much energy on doing the deal at the expense of post-merger planning
- Lack of clear responsibilities, leading to post-merger conflicts
- Insufficient research about the merger partner or acquired organization related to the workforce and cultural impact
- Too narrow a focus on internal issues to the neglect of the customers and the external environment
- Underestimating the problem of skills transfer or role changes
- Demotivation of employees
- Job fit and job satisfaction considerations

After the transaction is complete, transitions, consolidation, or change plans are developed. Here are a few ways ONA can accelerate these plans.

- Identifies the key players who are important to gain commitment to the changes (change agents)
- Identifies key risk areas that will slow or prevent integration
- Identifies leverage points to speed up integration
- Protects the investment and business objectives
- Identifies the key people that impact the organization and how
- Identifies or supports decisions for defining the organization structure
- Identifies how the organization really functions and gets the work done
- Identifies who should be more connected, how to connect people who aren't

ONA Assists with Risk Assessment

How might risk assessment in an M&A situation play out in the real world? Let's look at these two examples that are part of two other stories included in the book. One from Chapter 6 and one from Chapter 9.

Example 1

The acquisition substory in Chapter 6 was about the healthcare company that had a new CEO. They had acquired the infusion company about three years before using ONA to identify change agents. Map 12 is shared here again with a bit more explanation related to a M&A focus.

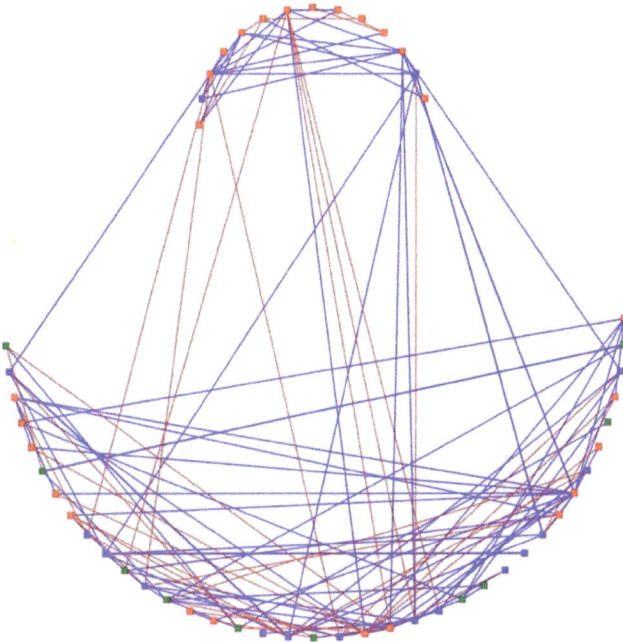

Map 12. Work Network.

The map represents the cross communication and information sharing in the Work Network after three years. The cluster of nodes at the top is the smaller acquired company. The cluster of nodes on the bottom is the larger medical equipment company that acquired the smaller company. The node colors represent the lines of business. All nodes are management level people, including executives.

There are a total of 18 possible leaders in the smaller acquired organization yet only 5 that are sharing information to work with the leaders in the larger company. There are a total of 49 leaders in the larger original core organization and only 14 who are sharing information to invite the newer acquired leaders into the core work environment. The CEO used the ONA results to share with all the leaders to grasp the situation and work with them to improve.

ONA and the visible story it produced explained the reality of how far integration had advanced—at least at the leadership level. The CEO specifically asked the leaders about the progress of the combined companies.

The leaders reported it was positive and working effectively. They said the company was fully integrated. Yet, the CEO admitted that there was a lot of work to do before they could confidently say they were one company now.

ONA is a good way to understand that leaders who make observations or decisions based only on their subjective experience or knowledge of what is happening, can end up making inaccurate ones. They do not have all the information and data of how their organization functions.

This information might answer the questions of why they had some of the organizational and people issues they were experiencing. Based on the consolidation map and lack of connections, the change agents are even more critical to their success as they move forward with the change initiative plans and focus on the integration.

Example 2

The second example is taken from the first responder organization in Chapter 9. The original organization acquired a smaller one about five years before using ONA.

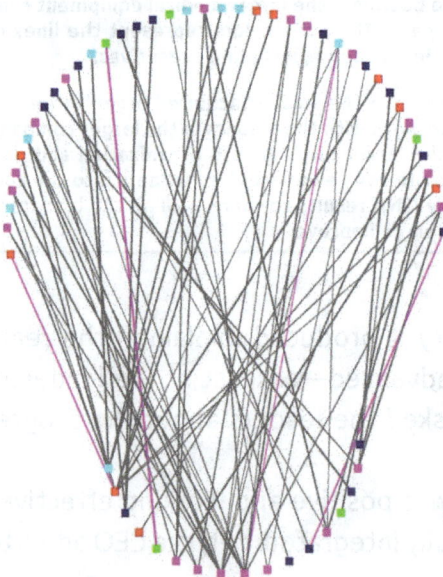

Map 16. Consolidation after Five Years (Combined Work and Improvement Networks).

- The colors represent their shift or assigned group/function designation.
- There were 42 employees in the acquired organization.
- There were 144 employees in the original organization before the acquisition.

More employees have been hired since, but this map only shows the original and acquired organization employees that have two-way connections in either the Work or the Improvement Networks. The gray lines represent connections in the Work Network. Pink lines represent connections in the Improvement Network that were not part of the Work Network connections.

ONA gave the leaders objective information to understand how the integration had progressed over five years. ONA changed the perception of the leaders and how they communicated about the acquisition. Had the leader known about ONA five years ago, the leader likely would have done the project then.

It would help him to know:

- Where best to place employees in the organization
- Who the key players were in both organizations
- How to get them on board more quickly
- What each culture looked like to identify where there is leverage or a challenge

However, it really is never too late. This organization is an example of that. Even though years have passed, there are some lingering issues left over or never addressed. ONA can uncover and help the organization leaders resolve issues to their benefit and those of the employees that they might not know about.

At a minimum, it raised the awareness of these leaders and they commented openly, "We need to change how we talk about the consolidation and the employees we are working with from that company. They have been doing their part. We are the ones that need to do more to include the members of the acquired organization into our culture."

9

EMERGING LEADERS, POWER BROKERS, CHANGE AGENTS, AND PATH FOR IMPROVEMENT

OVERVIEW

Problem: There was general employee dissatisfaction. There would be a change in leadership when the executive leader retired in a year.

Why: The leaders wanted to understand their organization issues to support the employees more and create positive change. It was imperative that the employees were engaged to support the organization mission.

What: The ONA survey was developed with a focus on the employees. Change agents, emerging leaders, and power connectors were identified. There was a focus on information sharing and how the structure influenced the results for this organization.

Outcome:

- ONA identified a mix of power connectors that indicated there were some untapped resources to create positive change going forward.

- ONA identified a process improvement option for improved employee satisfaction and involvement.
- ONA validated the consolidation from five years before as better than expected, from the leaders' perspective.
- Some individuals identified as key influencers were supported for promotion using ONA as part of the data analysis.

Getting Started

The leader from Chapter 7 shared the results of his organization's ONA experience at a conference. One of the attendees at the conference approached me after my presentation and eventually they opted to use ONA. Their purpose was to create positive change to address employee unrest, prepare for a new leader to be selected soon, and to build leadership skills for the emerging leaders.

The organization included about 250 employees in the ONA survey. There were essentially two major functions for this organization overall. One focused on Operations and the functional job categories associated with that. The other focused on first responder responsibilities and all functions associated with that.

The leader that contacted me was responsible for the first responder employees in the organization. The first responders included most of the employees and were a big responsibility. Based on the current morale concerns, he knew that it would be important to involve some of the employees in the decision and plan to get started with the ONA project.

He organized a committee of representative employees from all parts of the organization to understand what ONA is and can do, and to support the project. Having an employee group was a great way to communicate what was happening and why. It was a collaborative experience and one I will use as a suggestion for other clients to follow.

The committee helped to develop trust and confidence in the process and understand how it would support their organization. That made a difference in acceptance, interest, and participation. It also demonstrated transparency so employees knew the results would be shared openly and not just with management.

The hardest part of the ONA project is the data collection because it involves all the employees. They must take the time to answer questions and interrupt their job duties. The committee opted to set up survey access in a conference room with about 12–15 laptops so a group of people could take it all at the same time. They scheduled shifts over three days to accommodate everyone's schedules.

The committee members explained upfront what the purpose was and made it easy for everyone to access and ask questions on the spot. In most cases, that went smoothly, and we learned where we can improve the next time. In the end, we achieved a 99% response rate.

About two weeks later, I shared the initial results first with the committee, with the next presentation slated for the leadership team. There were a lot of questions and we developed context, priorities, and next steps together.

One of the main findings, which I already shared, is Example 2 in Chapter 8 for Mergers and Acquisitions. The same map is repeated below (see Map 16). It represents a combined view of the Work and Improvement Networks.

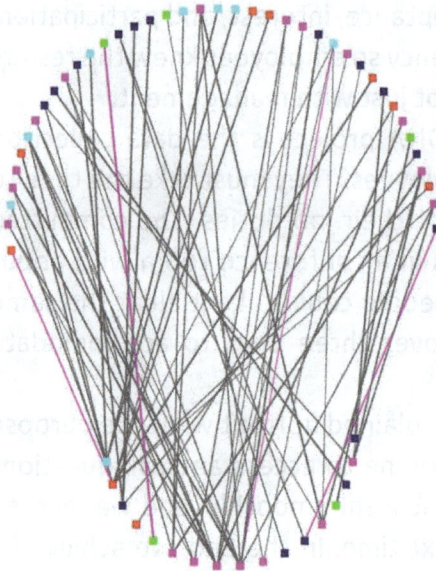

Map 16. Consolidation after Five Years (Combined Work and Improvement Networks).

This view of the Consolidation progress after five years serves two purposes.

1. It demonstrates that the consolidation is further along than the leaders thought it would be. Their intuition was that the acquired organization was still somewhat separate from the original core organization and resisted consolidation.

2. The gray lines show the work relationships and information flow between the two organizations. The pink lines show four individuals in both organizations that don't share work information but do share improvement ideas about workflow. These indicate higher trusted relationships between those employees.

The leaders can invite employees to participate more and integrate the two organizations to build the core network for resiliency. I combined the two networks to make the relationship between the Work and Improvement Networks clear. I designed the network questions to work together for the objective of this organization.

- The node colors represent their shift or assigned group/function designation.
- The acquired organization is on the bottom and the original, core organization is on the top.
- The gray lines represent connections in the Work Network.
- Pink lines represent connections in the Improvement Network that were not already connections in the Work Network.

- The pink lines are important to note since they are individuals discussing improvement ideas to strengthen the core. They would be the first people to tap to promote more integration ideas.

The Work Network question was: *"We interact with others to get our jobs done. Some people we interact with regularly, others on a case-by-case basis. Who do you regularly interact with on your job?"* The Work Network displays how the organization functions and where organizational knowledge is beginning to build.

The improvement question was a follow-up to the Work Network. The Improvement Network relies on employees to know what work processes, procedures, or methods exist and might be improved for efficiency or performance.

The Improvement Network question was: *"During your day-to-day tasks and interactions you sometimes discover new and better ways to do things. With whom do you work with to fix something that is broken like a procedure or process to overcome obstacles, and improve the flow of information/work?"*

Metrics Add Clarity

In addition, I included the metric analysis to explain more about who was reaching across the two groups to communicate and share information. The table below includes the "Post" employees, which are the new hires after the consolidation was technically complete.

The focus for this discussion is on the "Pre" and "Consol" groups. The Pre represents the original core organization that acquired a smaller private company. The Consol represents the acquired organization. Post employees are new employees and not included on Map 16. They weren't part of either organization during the acquisition.

- Count of links between the PRE integration organization and the CONSOL (consolidated post integration) organization.

- Higher negative ratios (in parentheses) indicate more interactions with their own group

- Higher positive ratios indicate more interactions outside their own group

- Balanced teams have a ratio closer to "0."

	Pre	Consol
Pre	350	62
Consol	62	46
Post	60	27
Ratio	(0.48)	0.32

The metrics shown in the chart indicate that the Consol employees are doing a better job of reaching across to the Pre employees than the Pre employees are to Consol employees. Even though five years had passed, there were good signs that the Consol employees continue to strive to be part of the organization.

The Consol employees showed initiative to share information and communicate with many of the employees in the Pre organization and make the effort to belong, communicate, and collaborate. This was important to the leaders, especially the leader retiring soon.

They appreciated having this confirmation and noted, "We need to change how we talk about the consolidation. We are the ones that need to do more to bring the members of the acquired organization into our culture." I also recommended that they include at least one of the leaders from the Consol organization in their leadership strategy and planning meetings. That would be a big step toward further consolidation.

Work Network

There is a required structure for this organization based on their industry, mission, and job requirements. That structure shows up in the Work Network and Decision Network. For this organization, it is expected that employees will work with the assigned people on their shift or based on their job function responsibilities.

There is some latitude of course, but I expected the colors to be grouped together according to the functions and/or shift assignments. In most cases, they were (see Map 17.) The Work Network is essentially about task relationships and transactions.

It doesn't require a high level of trust to complete a task. However, organizational knowledge begins in the Work Network. Relationships start to form as people get to know each other through functional relationships. They decide who they can work with effectively, trust, and want to work with in other ways, such as to make improvements.

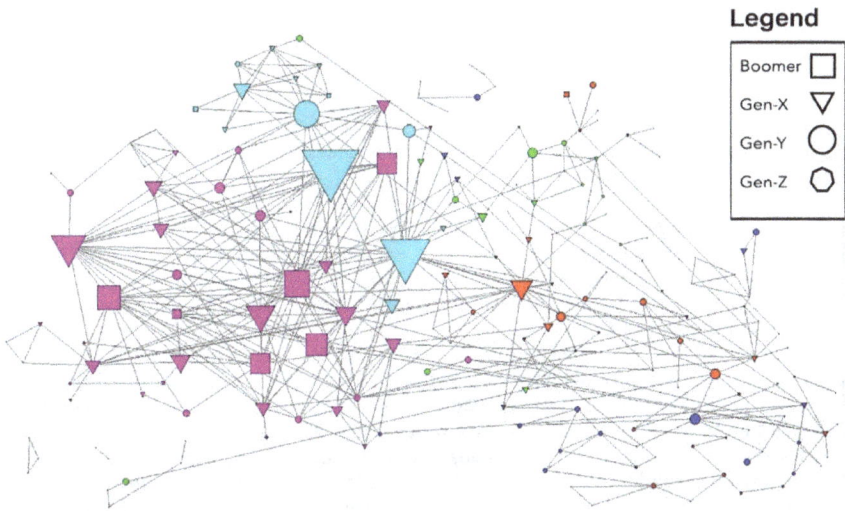

Legend

Boomer	☐
Gen-X	▽
Gen-Y	◯
Gen-Z	◯

Map 17. The Work Network.

- Colors represent functional groups.
- The clusters of colors follow the organization structure.
- Executive leadership are members of the aqua and the pink groups.
- The first responder group is represented by red, blue, and green nodes.
- The Operational functions are represented by pink and aqua nodes.

Legend

Boomer □
Gen-X ▽
Gen-Y ○
Gen-Z ○

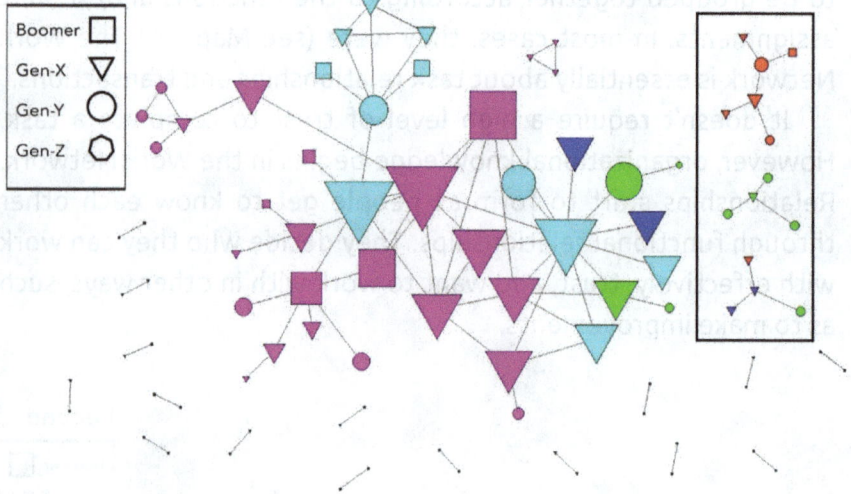

Map 18. The Improvement Network.

- The Improvement Network is a higher trust network.
- Shapes indicate generations.
- Colors indicate functions/shifts.
- The different size nodes indicate who has the best access and visibility to what flows in the network.
- There were fewer connections in this network, which was expected.
- The interesting part are the three smaller clusters of nodes outlined on the right side of the map. There is also a separate triangle at the top and several pairs of nodes separated from the core that line the bottom.
- Based on the size of the shapes, improvement ideas are decided in the higher-level leadership positions who reside in the pink and aqua functions.
- There were a lot of ideas generated among the red, green, and blue nodes that are not part of leadership and separated from the core network—the three clusters on the right side of the map together in the box.
- When they are separated from the core like this, they don't have a path or connection they trust to take their ideas forward to decision makers and get them implemented or even recognized.

When I met with the committee members they asked, "Some of us are in groups separated on the right. What does that mean in this network?"

I explained, "This network is telling us who is coming up with ideas to make changes to improve work processes, procedures, and efficiency. There are a lot of ideas generated in these smaller groups where people trust each other to share their ideas. However, when they are separated from the core like this, they don't have a path or connection they trust to take their ideas forward to decision makers and get them implemented or even recognized."

They realized this was becoming an issue and could be contributing to the employee unrest that initiated the ONA. As a result, the leader of the first responder groups organized a method for ideas to be submitted to lower levels who were now empowered to implement them.

This gave them an avenue to share their ideas and get them implemented to make a difference. When we do another ONA, I anticipate the gaps in this network will likely be closed. They are already implementing ideas using this new process.

Emerging Leaders and Change Agents

Another important outcome for this organization was to identify the emerging leaders and change agents. The emerging leaders were especially important. The first responder leader planned to use the social capital indicators for those who were applying for promotions or to identify people that he might not know about yet who were critical employees.

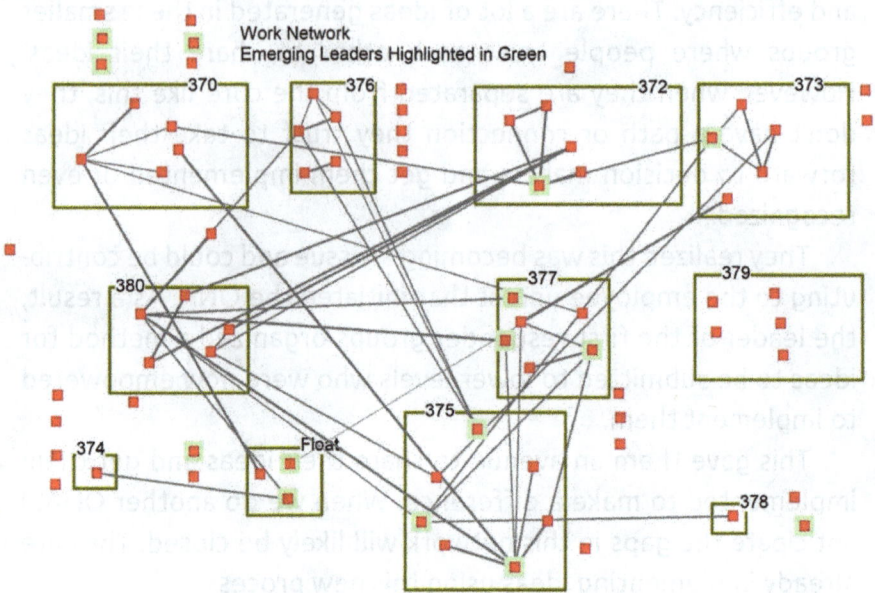

Map 19. Emerging Leaders for one part of the first responder group.

Map 19 shows the employees grouped by shifts with the emerging leaders highlighted in green. This map can be referenced when the person is promoted or moved around in the organization. It will identify who will be affected when that individual is moved to another part of the organization. It also will identify who the promoted person is directly connected to so they can quickly transfer knowledge or connect with others.

For the change agents, I provided a rank order list. The change agents are most important when there is any major change, such as when the new leader starts or if there is a restructuring. The change agents help communicate the importance and details of the change, so others are informed and supporting the change. A Change Agent Team (CHAT©) could be organized to coordinate the communication about the change.

This organization also plans to conduct an employee opinion survey. The questions can be designed according to any issues or areas where they would like more information. The opinion survey will be anonymous so I cannot do a direct correlation with the ONA results. However, I can use it to fill in some information that ONA identified and offer solutions based on some of the employee comments and suggestions.

The organization plans to conduct an ONA on a regular basis to measure change. When the new executive leader is identified, the ONA information will give them valuable insights about the organization. It will be their decision to use ONA going forward.

PART THREE:

USING ONA IN YOUR ORGANIZATION

10

ONA IMPLEMENTATION

THIS CHAPTER WILL explain the steps of an ONA project, so you have an idea of the time and resource commitment involved to get started using an Active ONA process. Active ONA uses a survey and includes all employees necessary to meet the objective and purpose.

Typically, an ONA project includes the entire organization. It can be more focused on the leaders only, department(s), or one part of the organization, for example based on a geographic location or a functional responsibility.

It is best to include as many employees as possible in the beginning and then take groups, departments, or functions out of the results, so you don't lose any relationship information. You can evaluate any of the demographics separately or use the data later as you uncover more information or want to get answers to other questions you develop as you learn more from the results.

Finding training and resources

When I do a project, most clients get involved and absorbed in the process and especially with the results. It is best to have the decision maker(s) directly involved as the project usually goes well when employees realize there is an engaged sponsor.

From a training perspective, we will work together and collaborate to achieve the goals you have for a project.

- I explain the analysis based on the results, the patterns of connections, and what they mean.
- I evaluate the relationship of the networks to each other and what the networks tell you.
- The analysis and results create the story of your organization and the system supporting it.

Today, there are many ONA options available that you can easily find on your own. There are many companies that sell the software they've created and who will train customers to do the analysis. However, that training supports their company's software design and how they do the analysis. Often, they have pre-defined network questions so the results are geared to support their software purpose.

In some cases, you can become a distributor using their software to promote their products and services. You can also hire them to do the project for you, which is how I work. I use software that I've purchased or licensed to create the surveys, analyze the connections, and create the graphs/maps. I use multiple software packages and am not restricted to the software vendor's method.

Using a consultant

Using a consultant is a great way to get started using ONA for your organization. If the project is a one-off, it is more cost effective to pay a consultant to be responsible from start to completion. Typically, clients are interested in learning about their organization more fully and prefer to have someone guide them through using ONA as a diagnostic tool. They usually do not have spare resources nor anyone trained in organizational behavior analysis using ONA.

It is important to have an objective analysis completed about how your organization functions. With a diagnostic like ONA, it is important to have someone who understands what the different patterns in the maps mean and how to use and interpret network metrics.

A trained professional knows:

- What to look for
- What organizational behavior can be understood from the results
- How the findings impact your plans and objectives
- How to act on the information and recommendations
- What to Look For

There are now quite a few consultants that do ONA-type projects for clients. In most cases, they belong to one of the distributor networks using a specific software tool they have designed. That can predefine how they will approach your project request.

For example, some vendors only look at three networks and use standard questions for every project which give a standard analysis methodology. For me, that is incomplete and ignores the nuance and uniqueness I have found with every client.

If you are considering hiring a consultant, it will save you money, time, and frustration if you ask them upfront about their process and what flexibility you would have working with them. Here are some ideas to consider if you are looking for a consultant. Ask them:

- How long they have been doing ONA work
- What types of projects they have done
- What outcomes they addressed with clients from the results
- Examples of recommendations or actions they or the client took based on the results
- What deliverables are included in a project

- How did they learn ONA and what background they have in data analysis and behavior in organizations, especially related to analyzing ONA results, metrics, patterns, etc.
- How they collect the data
- What types of network questions do they ask—are they predefined and standard, or flexible?

That is enough to decide if you want to work with them. I included the last bullet because I have seen some wild questions asked for ONA. For example, "Who do you gossip with?" Or, "Please indicate how much you like each person."

These are not appropriate questions and will not get truthful responses. The survey and results are not anonymous, and people can opt out of the survey. These types of questions create angst and distrust of the objective, and will impact the credibility of ONA.

There could already be a culture of fear or retribution and these questions would only confirm that. As an Industrial Organizational Psychologist, I am sensitive to what questions to include and to protect the confidentiality of the results as much as possible.

I want people to enjoy participating and not feel the results will be used in a punitive manner. If they are going to be used punitively, I will decline the opportunity to work with that organization. The results produce deep, broad, and rich information that all employees can benefit from learning. Respect the integrity of the process and don't abuse it.

Warning

ONA is a sophisticated tool that includes a depth and breadth of information about how your organization functions and can identify key contributors. Decision makers are advised to use it for awareness, growth, support, and development of the organization for improved effectiveness and an understanding of the system functionality.

If there are poor performers or negative influencers, you likely already know who they are. That needs to be addressed separately and not from the information gained using ONA. If you look for reasons to use the data in a negative way, it opens the door for misuse and gives ONA and you a bad reputation. It will make it much harder to get people to take any type of survey if their honest responses are not respected.

Preparing for an ONA project

It is best to survey the entire organization, if possible, to have all the data to work with upfront. That way you ask for employee involvement only once. The data can be used for some time for deeper analysis or to correlate with other data.

You can decide later to look at a particular department, the leaders, or other segments of the organization. It is much easier to analyze smaller groups or subsets from the entire dataset than go back and add them in later. Adding them in later is not advised since those that have already taken the survey won't have the new list of names available for their answers.

Typically, the boundary of the network is the organization/company. However, you can also include customers, vendors, or suppliers or other external participants that are important to know about and include in some way. It depends on the purpose of the project and why external connections are important.

You can create a general category for external nodes to be included. They don't necessarily have to take the survey themselves, but it is useful to know how many of your participants access those nodes and for what reason. I have had clients who reach out to external departments for expertise or because that is who they work with on a regular basis.

For example, in Chapter 5, the engineers were interacting frequently with customers and that was unusual. However, the

CEO was unaware of how many engineers were impacted until the ONA showed a one-way connection. As a result, he included customer service training for some of them and changed that responsibility for others.

Another major consideration is to ensure you have support from a key decision-maker. In my case, they are usually the person that requests the project, but not always. In that case, I work with my contact and ask that the key decision-maker be informed and part of the initial meeting.

It is important that they grasp what is involved and why they need to support it. They are usually the person that sends out an initial communication email to all employees to explain why it is important for everyone to participate. So it is critical that they understand and support it themselves.

Implementing the Project

Below are the steps to complete an Active ONA project with details of each step.

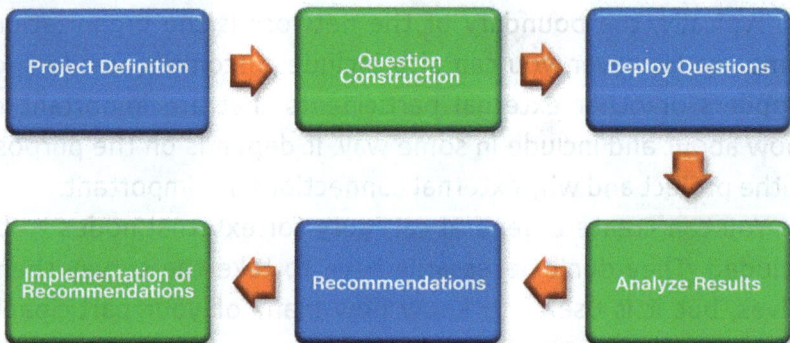

- Project Definition – This includes the initial discussion with the organization leaders/decision-makers who want to do the ONA project. You likely have some objective in mind or an issue to find out more about and resolve. The initial meeting is usually to:

a. Understand what deliverables you will get from the analysis and results
b. Understand your access to the results and analysis (report, PowerPoint, or both)
c. Understand what is included based on your objective for the ONA project
d. Understand the time commitment involved
e. Understand what part you will play

I offer suggestions and work with you to gain information to define the scope for your requirements and meet expectations. I explain we want to achieve a 100% response rate if possible. At a minimum, 85% is needed to ensure the metrics and data are valid for the analysis.

Project Start

Once you decide to move forward, there are preliminary steps that include your involvement.

1. A spreadsheet of all employees that will participate in the survey. The spreadsheet must have their first and last name and their email address as a minimum requirement.
2. The spreadsheet can also include any demographic information. I don't have to ask those questions in the ONA survey if they are included upfront.
3. Demographic information typically includes tenure, location, title, supervisor/manager, department, gender, and company (if there are multiples).
4. I prefer to get diverse information if HR approves to include DOB and ethnicity. I use DOB to sort them into

generation groups. I will include any demographic available or your preferences.

5. Some of the demographics are used to understand how inclusive the work environment is and can be compared to turnover statistics and other HR DEI implications.

- Question Construction – I develop a draft of ONA survey questions to get started and pick questions that support the objectives of the ONA project. Each question equates to a different network for the analysis. There is typically a range of four to eight questions included. There can be fewer or more, depending on the project objective.

For example, when I did the communication analysis for the CEO in Chapter 4, that was one specially designed question. I have done one to two questions for non-profit, member organizations as well. For example, I created special questions for the local chapters of ICF, IMC, and the SHRM chapter organizations.

Here are some example questions with the associated network for each:

➢ Work: We interact with others to get our jobs done. Some people we interact with regularly, others on a case-by-case basis. Who do you regularly interact with on your job?

➢ Expertise: Who do you consult on the deep technical aspects to complete your job?

➢ Improvement: With whom do you discuss what products, services, and technology are new or innovative in the industry and how they can be best applied to your organization's needs and goals?

➢ Advice: Whom do you seek out for advice on navigating the rough waters of work you are assigned to? This would be a person with experience in the organization that you can use as a sounding board or a source of wise counsel.

- Deploy Questions – Once the first two steps are complete, I set up the online survey. So far, the commonly available survey platforms, like Survey Monkey, are not conducive to ONA data collection. The survey question design for ONA is somewhat unique and the data must be separated into a node file and a link file. Each file has a standard format to be accepted into the specific software tool used. The software tool dictates the required format.

The survey software has many ONA features included. There are unique survey invitation links sent to the participants that cannot be shared. If some people do not have email, the survey software includes a general access link that can be accessed on a common computer.

If that won't work, it is possible to fill out a paper survey and the responses can be manually entered into the survey software. I try not to do that if possible since there are more chances for errors.

Launch Survey

Once the survey is set up, it is time to launch the project. I work with you to develop and determine:

a. The initial communication message that includes the purpose of the project
b. How we will use the data going forward
c. How/if the employees are involved
d. What feedback/information employees will receive
e. The time frame involved

I emphasize the importance of everyone's participation and the goal to get as close to 100% response as possible. To date, I have never gotten less than a 94% response rate for any project

I have done, except for the non-profit member associations. That makes sense as they often do not have active members.

It is important for employees to understand this is not an anonymous survey. They will have a list of names to pick from to populate their network choices and respond to each question. The results can remain confidential, but that must be decided upfront and shared with the employees in the communication messages. Confidential means the data is only shared with a select group and/or the maps do not have names.

Usually, the survey remains open for two weeks, depending on the client and how their organization functions. I send out reminders to only those who have not completed the survey. Sometimes, the client is involved and sends out reminders as well.

- Analyze Results – Once the survey closes, I download and begin analyzing the data. I look for patterns of collaboration, communication, and information flows, and the similarities and/or differences among the networks and groups of nodes.

I analyze the metrics and begin looking deeper into the organization at a more micro level. Unless I have worked with the organization before, I know very little about the context or who the individuals are and if their function is important to the organization.

The names mean very little to me until the data explains more about groups, departments, individuals, or what is measured. I develop lists of key roles and patterns or anomalies that show up. I review all the data with the project objectives in mind.

Examples include lists of change agents, emerging leaders, power connectors, and key influencers. In some cases, I develop 'ego networks' of individuals, usually leaders. These individual networks show their particular networks of who is directly connected to them (based on the network) and two steps out—who is connected to those who they are connected to as well.

There is a list of the key findings and a PowerPoint presentation with the important networks and information. The process tells a story or provides insight to understand the organization system. The maps are the visual explanation and provide any additional details that might be important. The metrics are included to support some of the analysis and give more in-depth meaning to interpreting the maps.

- Results/Recommendations – I include initial findings for context and review. I often have more questions than answers since the findings are based solely on the data analysis, and I need context to support any firm conclusions.

Sometimes the maps can be difficult for people to understand so I use a build process to get them used to seeing the layout and help them understand how it fits together. It is important to have someone with experience in understanding organizational behavior, relationships, and what the pattern of interactions means. The maps can be complex and nuanced with rich information. Data analytics alone is not enough.

As we go through them, there is a lot of discussion and questions. I leave with a better understanding of what is important and what interests them to take action. I adjust the initial results based on the feedback to create a final presentation.

Recommendations are based on the final analysis. The recommendations can be used as the next steps and to develop more detailed action plans. The recommendations offer ideas of how to use the data. They also might include how to resolve an issue that was identified in the analysis or the discussion about the initial results.

- Implementation of Recommendations – This is an optional step. You might use the recommendations to develop and implement your own action plans. If there is something specific you can't or don't want to do, I can continue additional work. It is possible to dig deeper into the data to provide more information or for another consultant to do work I don't feel qualified to do.

Once you see what ONA can do, you will be energized as you understand your organization in a different way. ONA will inspire you to be creative and find solutions to problems you have been concerned about or for which you now have answers that you didn't have before.

For example, in Chapter 9, based on the results from the improvement network, the first responder leader created a way for non-leaders to be empowered and implement new ideas that employees shared.

> *ONA is a complex tool that if used properly can diagnose many causes of workplace challenges. Without it, leaders are left chasing the symptoms.*

ONA is a powerful diagnostic tool that opens the door to solutions that stick. There are few other tools that compare. As I mentioned before, an X-ray doesn't provide the solution for a doctor. They use it to figure out the solution(s). ONA is the same. It doesn't offer answers upfront, like a behavioral assessment report might provide.

ONA is a complex tool that if used properly can diagnose many causes of workplace challenges. Without it, leaders are left chasing the symptoms. They think they are addressing the causes, much like the CIO in Chapter 2. Even the CEO and HR VP in Chapter 5 initially made those assumptions, which were in error and created turnover risk.

Time Commitment

The chart below provides a visual of how much time commitment is involved overall and for your employees. It is difficult to judge the exact time commitment from the graph. That will depend on availability of resources involved and how quickly people respond to the survey.

A guide to use is that if there are about 100 employees participating in the survey, it will take about 10 minutes of their time to complete the survey. The more employee names to sort through and pick from, the more time it will take.

Steps one and two are usually quick since I facilitate the discussion and guide you through the process and what is required. What often lags are to get the spreadsheet, edit it for proper format, and ensure we have all the demographics included.

The results session for the initial draft review typically lasts an hour to gain understanding and gather context. The results are updated for final review to any number of audiences.

Total calendar time is around six weeks. Results may be available much sooner, but there might be many changes and questions to address.

Here is an overview of the steps and the time involved for each participant level.

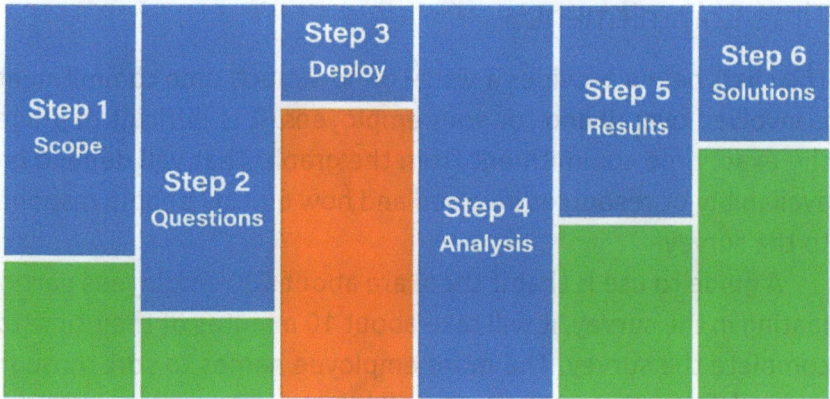

Legend

Seity Contribution	
Client Contribution	
Employee Time	

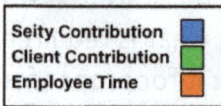

Reading the Results

As I go through the initial findings, I walk you through the descriptive statistics of the project:

- How many people responded
- The response percentage rate
- How many networks were included and analyzed
- How many networks are included in the presentation
- A list of the initial findings
- Any metrics that stand out from the analysis

The initial findings offer a good sense of how your organization really functions. You will see who the key people are that make a difference in your organization. ONA can either validate or refute anything you might have thought about your organization.

Often, many unknowns are discovered or there are surprises about a group, or a person, or a situation. I pointed out a lot of these in the chapter stories.

ONA data is rich, deep, broad, and nuanced. The examples of some of this were shared in the stories so listing them now won't have the same meaning. There isn't a defined list of results or expectations when you start the ONA. There are categories of information that do come from the analysis. Such things as the key influencers, emerging leaders, change agents, and others.

CONCLUSION

Action is Critical to Success

ONA is a diagnostic. It doesn't produce a list of action steps to take from the analysis alone. That is up to the interpretation and skill of the consultant or person doing the ONA project to meet your project objectives.

Many consultants decline to help with action plans as they only want to do the ONA portion. I use ONA to start the relation-ship and don't stop after I complete the ONA portion. For me, that is the beginning of discovery so I can support you with the action plans as well, if it is something I am qualified to do.

> *It is important to act once you understand what ONA provides. You are doing a disservice to your employees and organization if you put it on a shelf without acting.*

ONA provides valuable information that, at a minimum, will help you understand your organization in a different way than before, and holistically. I discuss with my clients that it is like any survey you ask of your employees. They take time to answer the questions and wonder why you are doing the survey and project.

They want to know what you are going to do with the results and if you will act. You are doing a disservice to your employees and organization if you stop and put it on a shelf without acting. Don't let it get stale before you act.

If you do act, you can measure your success and see the change and impact it had when you do another ONA later. ONA makes the invisible visible for you to act. You can continue watching your organization evolve if you take these snapshots on a regular basis.

There are many ways to take the results forward. You can:

- Solve problems with confidence and data
- Meet challenges that you have been facing
- Find leverage points in the organization you never knew you had
- Learn about key employees you might not know about
- Build a resilient and effective organization
- Create a competitive advantage
- Increase the potential for engaged and satisfied employees that enhance the culture
- Improve performance management processes, retention, and organizational effectiveness
- Much, much more

If you have new leaders in your organization, use the results and presentation to help onboard them quickly. They will appreciate learning about the organization in an objective way and seeing how people relate to one another. They can develop priorities for who they want to meet with, questions to ask, and get up to speed with some foundational knowledge that reduces the learning curve.

Use the knowledge you have about key influencers and change agents to onboard new employees more quickly. That will socialize them into your culture and connect them to individuals who will help them feel like they belong. It will increase the chance that they will want to stay and help to lower your turnover rates.

Use the key influencers, power connectors, and change agents to share information and build your organization as you want for improved effectiveness and positive change. Add the social capital information to your succession plans, development processes, and performance management process. Get the full picture of the employee value each person holds and contributes to your organization.

Don't accept things at face value. Take the time to complete an ONA diagnostic to confirm your intuition or discover new information you didn't know about. Use the objective data to make decisions, create positive change, support your employees, and listen to what their behavior is telling you.

If you think you know how your organization functions based on your intuition, *turn intuition into science* using ONA to know for sure. It makes your organization visible and fills in the white space on the org chart, so you know how the work really happens. Then act!

Review Inquiry

Hey, it's Deborah here.

I hope you've enjoyed the book, finding it both useful and fun. I have a favor to ask you.

Would you consider giving it a rating wherever you bought the book? Online book stores are more likely to promote a book when they feel good about its content, and reader reviews are a great barometer for a book's quality.

So please go to the website of wherever you bought the book, search for my name and the book title, and leave a review. If able, perhaps consider adding a picture of you holding the book. That increases the likelihood your review will be accepted!

Many thanks in advance,

Deborah Peck

Would You Like Deborah Peck to Speak to Your Organization?

Book Deborah Now!

Deborah Peck accepts a limited number of speaking engagements each year. To learn how you can bring her message to your organization, email dpeck@seity.com or visit http://www.seity.com and fill out the contact form.

ACKNOWLEDGMENTS

This book would never have happened without all those who supported me on my journey when starting a new career as an industrial/organizational psychologist. Most of those mentioned are unaware that I wrote a book, but they still had a big part. Those who supported me to develop and grow in the work that I do have made it possible for me to share these stories with you.

Family

My immediate family, dad, mom, and brother have all passed. I believe they would be proud and happy to know I wrote this book. My dad knew about it before he passed. He was excited to know I was writing a book. He was my hero and I only hope I gave to him as much as he gave to me.

My husband, Keith, and son, Ryan, have been on the journey with me in many ways—some by choice and some because of the choices I made that necessitated their involvement in some way.

I am so grateful to Keith for being open-minded about my career choices and supporting me through challenging times. He sacrificed in ways I probably don't even know about to give me the opportunity to fulfill my dream. He played a key part in building my business and shared his resolve to help me overcome the challenges. He listened to many stories about my experiences when I needed to have someone to work through my thoughts and find ways to move forward.

Ryan was there with us at the kitchen table years ago, fully engaged in picking the company name when we launched Seity, Inc. He was very young at the start but always so interested and supportive. He still is today. He is now a young, brilliant, kind, and compassionate man. I trust and admire him completely. I am so grateful to be blessed with a child that has so much to offer the world. He is on his own journey, and I support him as he has always done for me. Thank you, Ryan, for being such a great son with common sense, solid values, and amazing creative ideas. I wish you a wonderful life and a fantastic career of your choice.

Friends and Colleagues

As I was starting out full time, I called upon a leader I worked with at American Express who was unlike most of the leaders there. John Vaszily was patient, caring, very business-wise, and served as a mentor and coach to me when I was assigned to a major corporate project that he led at AMEX. I reconnected with him to see what he thought of my new career. I had a solid reputation in technology, but not as an I/O psychologist.

He was critical to my growth and became my first corporate client. He helped me develop as a consultant and gave me great opportunities to demonstrate that this was the right decision for me to pursue. He jumped in the deep end with ONA as well and that was the start. I knew then that this was for me.

My friend and colleague, Janet Young, was a major influence on me during this time. She was supportive and gave me opportunities to meet people and tag along to events where she was helping. Janet had a background in organizational change management and organizational effectiveness techniques. She coached me generously and patiently.

Janet helped me put together an executive forum to launch my business full time in 2009. With the downturn in the economy, this was not an easy goal, but we did it! We got 40 companies and 120 people to come and learn about power networks in organizations and ONA. Thank you, Janet, for your generosity, time, dedication, coaching, and interest in ONA. I could never have managed the launch without you or grown as a consultant without the great tools you shared and your insight.

Janet introduced me to Dr. Mary O'Hara Devereaux, a well-known business forecaster and consultant. Dr. Devereaux knew about ONA and had a chapter in her book about it. She generously agreed to be the keynote speaker at the Forum. She was the reason people came to the event and I am grateful to both Janet and Mary for that kick start and support. Thank you, Mary, for supporting my start and your interest in ONA. You energized my thinking about the importance of applying ONA in the workplace to develop solutions from the results.

Another important relationship that developed over the years was with Koko Tzavaras. I met Koko at a networking event for women. Koko is the best executive recruiter. We became friends and colleagues and supported each other. She made introductions for me and gave me many opportunities to present my work to business professionals. Thank you, Koko, for the endless hours we spent discussing opportunities and challenges we faced, and for your positive, common-sense view of relationships.

Koko introduced me to Leathers Milligan. Leathers Milligan was a well-known coaching and outplacement services company. It had just been sold to a new owner when I met them. One of the remaining founders, Jack Milligan, was at the head of the table when I presented ONA. I mentioned Jack in the preface. He coined the phrase that I used for the title of my book.

I was fortunate to meet Denise Gredler, the CEO and Founder of Best Companies AZ. Denise knows just about everyone and is a connector to many businesses. She is very creative and just a great person. We eventually started a business relationship and still work together today. She has been very supportive of all that I do. Thank you, Denise, for always believing in me and the introductions you have made for me. Denise offered to read a few chapters of my book to give me feedback as well.

I have met many people who have contributed to my success and growth. Kim Kressaty is someone I met by chance when she worked for Dr. George Land. Kim immediately understood the value of ONA. She is a great thought leader that helped me think through challenging opportunities and offered creative suggestions. Thank you, Kim, for being there during some of the hardest times I faced along the way. Kim was a key contributor on my book editorial committee to give me unvarnished feedback.

I am grateful to Sara Fleury who was a consultant for one of my clients when we met. Sara is a very talented PR and Communications professional who is just a fun person. She was supportive as I was introduced to the CEO and others to conduct an ONA.

Linda Scorzo, the CEO and owner of Hiring Indicators, hired me as a sub-contractor to support the development, maintenance, and credibility of the Reveal assessment her company designed, developed, and produced. She hires I/O psychologists to support the assessments to ensure validity, reliability, and production value to her clients. Thank you, Linda, for your kindness, support, patience, and insight. You were generous of your time to read my book and offer great feedback that helped me gain clarity.

From that relationship, I also got to know Autumn-Lynn Fabrizi. Autumn-Lynn makes work fun. She is a very talented graphic designer who supports Hiring Indicators. She has been supportive of my work. She took the maps and other charts for the book and made them more appealing and standard to meet the publishing requirements. Thank you, Autumn-Lynn, for who you are and the great work you do. Not to mention, just being there.

Mentors

When I first started learning there was a method to analyze how people interact and form relationships in the workplace, I thought it was very similar to what I did as a data network engineer. It was similar, except that data networks didn't form trust or base their connections on altruistic or even selfish reasons.

After researching and learning what I could on my own, I became convinced that the data, analysis, and information ONA produced was valuable to organizations and leaders. I intuitively knew about these connections but had no idea they could be analyzed objectively. There were interactive patterns that told stories or identified problems and solutions to those problems.

I spent time learning as much as I could on my own, but it wasn't enough. I had to learn from experts that were developing research, software, metrics, and tools that I could use. I found some free software that could analyze networks and produce graphical displays. I wanted something that was more specific to working with organizations and identifying trust since my dissertation included trust as the topic.

My research brought me to Orgnet and Valdis Krebs. He has a fascinating story about his own journey, but his background and education also brought him to SNA/ONA. He served as a coach, educator, creative thinker, thought leader, and expert that I could learn from.

When I contacted Valdis, he quizzed me about my background and purpose for requesting to buy his software. He was "picky" about who he sold his software to and asked how I would use it. He explained that he developed InFlow himself and purposefully for business users. That was the right software for me to use. Valdis offers coaching and consulting support for those that purchase his software. I learn something new from every project I have done, but especially having Valdis to look at it from his perspective.

During my search and journey, I uncovered another name that caught my eye as someone to approach. Dr. Karen Stephenson is an anthropologist. Her perspective as an anthropologist is to look at systems in organizations. I liked that approach.

She was not easy to contact but eventually announced she was offering her methodology to the Organizational Development Network (ODN). I was a member and signed up for the first cohort. That turned into a three-year experience with many great relationships among the cohort and experiences as we learned together. I am grateful to have learned from an expert who took a different approach to the analysis.

Book Support

I also want to thank the content editorial committee who were kind enough to read my manuscript and give me honest feedback and suggestions to improve. Kim Kressaty is mentioned again here, Kim Rhule whom I met during the Dr. Stephenson days, and my husband Keith Peck. Denise Gredler and Linda Scorzo offered to read it and gave me great feedback and suggestions as well.

A special acknowledgement to my writing coach, Cathy Fyock. She was patient with me as there were many interruptions, known as "life happens," along the way. She never gave up on me and was always supportive. I knew when she advised me on something, it was based on wisdom and experience. I didn't question her guidance. I am so grateful that we crossed paths when we did. I might never have made it to publication otherwise.

Clients

The clients that I have worked with have been so valuable to my learning and to applying what I love to do—supporting them to make their organizations effective and productive. I won't name them since many of them have stories in this book and I want to respect their anonymity. However, they know who they are, and I am grateful for the trust they gave me to work closely with them, their leaders, and their employees.

Everyone mentioned and countless others that I have crossed paths with have helped me fulfill my vision—to contribute my work to my community and beyond. Perhaps this book will have a small impact on positive change for growth in organizations and the ability to increase their effectiveness. I offer it for organizational health to any leader interested in finding that.

ABOUT THE AUTHOR

Deborah Peck, Ph.D., President and Founder of Seity Insight, Inc., works with organizations and leaders to address communication, collaboration, retention, engagement, innovation, and other challenges in the workplace using Organizational Network Analysis (ONA). She has been called "The Business Doctor" because of her scientifically oriented approach, using effective tools and methods in her work. She holds a B.S. in Business Management and Computer Science and earned a Ph.D. in Industrial/Organizational Psychology. She has been featured in *Scottsdale at Work*, *The Suit*, and *Arizona Women*, and was among the top 10 Assessment Consulting Companies for 2020 featured in *HR Tech Outlook*. She is sought out as a speaker for workforce, people analytics, and human capital conferences.

She has a broad background in business practices, technology, leadership, consulting, coaching, and understanding workplace behavior. She has decades of experience in business and data network engineering, venture funded start-ups, and Fortune

100 companies across multiple industries. She held ascending leadership positions in many companies and industries before starting her consulting practice. Her experience and education influence her systems perspective and learning organization techniques, providing a foundation for her consulting practices to create optimal business results and improve effectiveness in any organization.

Seity Insight focuses on Organizational Network Analysis (ONA) and Workplace Assessments to "turn intuition into science." Our "why" at Seity is that we aim to support leaders as they heal their organizations. Seity does this through awareness using scientific methods, objective data, and analysis that address challenges and develop solutions that stick. The solutions produce results to lower turnover, increase engagement and productivity, and improve communication, collaboration, and customer service, as well as reduce silos to align the organization for improved effectiveness. This empowers leaders and businesses to address the issues they face and capitalize on their most important assets, their people, while improving their bottom line.

Deborah can be reached at: www.seity.com

www.ingramcontent.com/pod-product-compliance
Lightning Source LLC
Chambersburg PA
CBHW071606210326
41597CB00019B/3419